The Novels of Ernest Hemingway

A Critical Study

ISHTEYAQUE SHAMS

ATLANTIC
PUBLISHERS & DISTRIBUTORS (P) LTD

Published by

ATLANTIC

PUBLISHERS & DISTRIBUTORS (P) LTD

7/22, Ansari Road, Darya Ganj, New Delhi-110002
Phones : +91-11-40775252, 23273880, 23275880, 23280451
Fax: +91-11-23285873
Web: www.atlanticbooks.com
E-mail: orders@atlanticbooks.com

Branch Office
5, Nallathambi Street, Wallajah Road, Chennai-600002
Phones : +91-44-64611085, 32413319
E-mail: chennai@atlanticbooks.com

Printed in India at Nice Printing Press, A-33/3A, Site-IV, Industrial Area, Sahibabad, Ghaziabad, U.P.

PREFACE

IT IS difficult to ignore or minimize the fact that a good deal has been written on Ernest Hemingway's life as well as on the various aspects of his writings. At the same time, it is also difficult to ignore or minimize the point that several editions of Hemingway's works have been published from time to time. All these publications of Hemingway's books, besides the critical books and papers on his writings, establish the fundamental fact that Hemingway has been a very popular writer and that his books have attracted readers in a large and still larger number. His popularity is not conditioned so much by his descriptions of sex and violence, travels and adventures in his books as by something that lies hidden behind the descriptions. Truly enough, Hemingway is a writer of a lost generation, of an era of chaos and disillusionment, but his approach is neither defeatist nor negative in nature; instead, it is something vigorously optimistic and positive in spirit. As we go through his writings, his novels and short stories in particular, we do find that there is a writer who looks upon life as a kind of struggle and challenge and who believes that in spite of all adverse situations, it is always better to get destroyed than to accept defeat. Moreover, this import of Hemingway's works is heightened and made richer and more meaningful and significant by the manner in which he brings it out. What Hemingway seeks to tell us through his books is indeed important, but far more important is the way, the mode in which he tells it. It is generally said that Hemingway writes in a very plain, simple and austere kind of style and that there is nothing involved or complex or ambiguous as such about his writing. However, as I went through his books, his novels and short stories in particular, I did realize that there was much to be explored and considered in order to be able to make a proper and adequate assessment of his linguistic capability.

ISHTEYAQUE SHAMS

CONTENTS

1

Perspectives on Hemingway

THERE IS perhaps great substance and meaningfulness in the statement that 'no other author of our time has had such a general and lasting influence on the generation which grew up between the World Wars as Ernest Hemingway.'[1] Hemingway's case as a writer is highly interesting for several reasons. The first of these reasons is that it is difficult to separate Hemingway, the man from Hemingway, the writer because most of his writings, in one way or another, relate directly to his personal life. Secondly, Hemingway, the writer has, in a striking way, his own bearing upon Hemingway, the man, for right from his early age he was determined to be a writer. Thirdly, Hemingway was so much a man of enterprise and action, of daring and adventure that in his lifetime he grew into a legend. And, lastly, we have to keep wondering as to how Hemingway who spent so much of his time over other pursuits and activities, could be able to write poems, plays, short stories and novels. As such, it would be proper and profitable to keep in view all these aspects of his colourful personality in order to be able to undertake an assessment, not only of his writings in general but also of the symbols in his novels in particular.

Ernest Hemingway, we all know, was rather a prolific writer; in fact, he had so shaped himself as to lose no opportunity to render his impressions and experiences into an articulate form. His first book entitled *Three Stories and Ten Poems* was published in 1923, and it was immediately followed by a collection of his stories called *In Our Time* in 1924. Two years later, that is, in 1926, Hemingway brought out two of his novels, the satirical short novel, *Torrents of Spring,* and *The Sun Also Rises.* At this point we cannot do without recalling that *The Sun Also Rises* achieved immediate success and was indeed acclaimed as a great work of fiction. His second volume of short stories, *Men Without Women* was published in 1927, and it was followed two years later by his second novel entitled A *Farewell to Arms.* In 1932 Hemingway brought out a book about bull-fighting named *Death in the Afternoon,* while the third volume of his short stories entitled *Winner Take Nothing* came out in 1933. He wrote a travelogue called *Green Hills of Africa* in 1935, while shortly thereafter he wrote two of his powerful short stories, 'The Short Happy Life of Francis Macomber' and 'The Snows of Kilimanjaro,' that emerged out of his experiences of prolonged hunting in Africa. The year 1936 saw the publication of his next novel, *To Have and Have Not.* Hemingway's play relating to the Spanish Civil War, captioned *The Fifth Column* came out in 1937. From 1940 to 1952 Hemingway wrote three novels named *For Whom the Bell Tolls* (1940), *Across the River and into the Trees* (1950) and *The Old Man and the Sea* (1952). It did not come to the world as a surprise that he received the Nobel Prize for literature in 1954. And equally so, there was nothing unusual about his shooting himself to death in 1961. *A Moveable Feast,* brought out posthumously in 1964, contains essays concerning Hemingway's years in Paris from 1921 to 1926.[2]

It is generally said that Ernest Hemingway was not merely a rebellious, an aggressive individual but also a manly writer, tough and virile, and that he may be looked upon as perhaps the manliest among the twentieth-century writers. Somehow or other, Ernest Hemingway, the man forced his way into growing as Ernest Hemingway, the legend, a legend in his very lifetime. However, in order to be able to understand and appreciate the real nature of his character, we have to examine the very course of his life in all its fullness and diversity. Although he had been born in a well-to-do middle-class family at Oak Park in Illinois, right from his childhood he was a victim of emotional tension arising out of the conflict between 'the spartan demands of his physician father'[3] and 'the rich artistic aura which his mother attempted to cast over her family.'[4] All the same, there were the grains of precocious wisdom in Hemingway. During his stay at the Oak Park School, it is true, he was interested as much in sports and outdoor activities as in acquiring learning; nevertheless, even as a boy, his zeal for writing was stimulated both by the nature of the school curriculum, with its emphasis on classical myths, narrative poems and novels, and by the particular gifts of two of his teachers, Miss Gibbs and Miss Dixon. Hemingway's first available stories, 'Judgement of Manitou,' 'A Matter of Colour' and 'Sepi Jingan,' written as a school student in 1916, deal with spying and revenge, and bring out his interest in Nature and violence. At Oak Park he was actively associated with the school magazine, *Tabula,* and the school newspaper, *Trapeze,* and what is really important about his school journalism is the fact that in this respect his model was Ring Lardner, an eminent columnist of the Chicago *Tribune*. Hemingway's 'High school fiction,' says Fenton, 'demonstrates that he was blessed with an acute interest in all new experiences, a ready narrative style, and a sound training in clear self-expression,'[5] and goes on to express that the 'rest would come only after a series of increasingly more sophisticated tutors and a vast amount of personal growth and application.'[6]

After his schooling, in his restlessness to move out of Oak Park, Hemingway decided to go in for journalism and became a reporter with the Kansas City *Star* which was a famous paper at that time in mid-west America. Hemingway was not just happy with his profession as a journalist; in fact, in the course of his day-to-day reporting he learned a good deal about the art of writing, particularly under the guidance of C.G. Wellington, Assistant City Editor of the paper, and Lionel Calhoun Moise who was closely associated with it. And though he worked as one of the Kansas City *Star* reporters for barely seven months, he regarded his stay there as a means to an end, and wrote several stories, the more important among them being 'A Pursuit

Race' and 'God Rest You, Merry, Gentlemen,' that are marked by the writer's flair for action, his understanding and appreciation of experiences, and his purposeful avoidance of sentimentality. In this connection Hemingway himself says:

> Those were the best rules I ever learned for the business of writing. I've never forgotten them. No man with any talent, who feels and writes truly about the thing he is trying to say, can fail to write well if he abides by them.[7]

And Charles A. Fenton states the very same thing in a difficult way:

> Literary critics have sometimes patronized Hemingway as the victim of an abbreviated and inadequate education. On the contrary, in addition to the admirable instruction given at Oak Park High School, he was the recipient of an extremely literate and concentrated training, general as well as vocational, on the *Star*. It was an education to which, like any young man, he would be more attentive than he would have been to similar instruction at, say, the University of Illinois.[8]

Hemingway's penchant for experiences and still newer experiences, his love for action, and his commitment to an effective use of the linguistic medium, these have been his outstanding traits as a writer of fiction right from his early years.

It is true that Hemingway felt interested in journalism, but he felt more interested in serving the cause of war victims, first because of his humanistic and altruistic ideals, and secondly because he viewed war as one of the reservoirs of experiences, and that is why he enlisted himself as a Volunteer in the Red Cross Ambulance Corps for Italy. Hemingway says:

> I thought...about what a great advantage an experience of war was to a writer. It was one of the major subjects and certainly one of the hardest to write truly of and those writers who had not seen it were always very jealous and tried to make it seem unimportant, or abnormal, or a disease as a subject, while, really, it was just something quite irreplaceable that they had missed.[9]

Hemingway joined his assignment in Italy in early 1918, but got seriously injured in trench warfare a few months later; all the same, even in the bewildering din and confusion of war, he kept on writing articles and short stories. Hemingway informs us:

> When you go to war as a boy you have a great illusion of immortality. Other people get killed; not you.... Then when you are badly wounded the first time you lose that illusion and you know it can happen to you. After being severely wounded.... I had a bad time until I figured it out that nothing could happen to me that had not happened to all men before me. Whatever I had to do men had always done.[10]

It is pretty evident that by 1918 itself, when Hemingway was only a nineteen-year old boy, he had acquired a personality and a role to perform in life.

Hemingway came back to America in 1919, and after nearly a year's stay at Oak Park and Michigan, proceeded to Canada to join the *Star Weekly* there at Toronto as a member of its editorial staff. Although crime and violence had a special fascination for him, it was 'as a humorist...that Hemingway presented himself in much of his *Star Weekly* material in 1920,'[11] and his 'style and attitudes matured as he ranged experimentally through the various levels of burlesque, mimicry, satire, and irony.'[12] It is important to note that even at the age of twenty-one, Hemingway could legitimately think of himself as a writer, and could also feel that, given time, he would earn a living through his works. He returned to Chicago in the autumn of 1920, and eventually became the associate editor of *Co-operative Commonwealth* there. His employment in Chicago was a monotonous affair; the duration of his stay there was by no means comparable to the seven months of his stay in Kansas City, nor to the period he had spent in Toronto, and still during this period he made definite contributions to his literary output. And even though during his stay in Chicago Hemingway developed a distaste for American insensitivity and provincial arrogance, he read a lot of Sherwood Anderson, wrote a good deal, got married and received an appointment as roving correspondent for the Toronto *Star* in Europe with headquarters in Paris.

Hemingway and his wife left for Europe at the beginning of 1922: 'A friend of mine and a very delightful man, Ernest Hemingway, and his wife,' writes Sherwood Anderson to Lewis Gelantiére on November 28, 1921, 'are leaving for Paris.'[13] During his trip to Europe, Hemingway visited Spain, Switzerland, Italy, Germany, Greece and France, and, besides attending to his journalistic duties, could acquire a host of impressions and experiences that helped him immensly as a creative writer. In Paris, his encounters with Gertrude Stein, Ezra Pound and James Joyce were productive in their own ways, for while Ezra Pound encouraged him to take up his vocation as a creative writer with due seriousness, in her turn, Gertrude Stein, the presiding deity of the literary association there, explained to him her conception of writing as concentration, as heavy, aching effort which was indeed something new for Hemingway and advised him to give up his job as a journalist. It was really fortunate that Hemingway had constantly resisted being merely a journalistic hack and had always aspired to become a creative writer. And though journalism did create many problems for him, it nevertheless, gave him, over the years, a finished maturity of prose and an interest in human situations, a penchant for authenticity of details, a determination to throw himself responsively into whatever atmosphere he was exploring, and a sardonic recognition of the tenuousness of established truths. Gertrude Stein's advice to him to give up journalism did ignite his growing impatience with newspaper work, and though he had been associated with journalism since 1916 right from his school-days at Oak Park, on his return from Europe to Toronto in the second half of 1923, he brought his journalistic career to an abrupt end at the beginning of 1924. Talking to Harvey Breit in 1950, Hemingway did very meaningfully observe: 'In writing I have moved through arithmetic, through plane geometry and algebra, and now I am in calculus.'[14]

Hemingway returned to Paris early in 1924, kept on writing short stories and novels as intense personal commitment, and it was nearly nine years later that he left Paris on a trip to Africa.

From his very boyhood days, Africa held a peculiar fascination for Hemingway, and this interest was further roused by the novel, *Batoula,* written by a Negro, René Maran. Although *Batoula* was basically a socio-political novel, Hemingway had considered it in 1922 only as a remarkably realistic description of life in an African village. Next to Africa, Spain too had its own fascination for him; he travelled to Spain four times during the Civil War, and advocated the cause of Spanish freedom fighters. In this connection Leo Lania says:

> Spain is Hemingway's great love. Africa represents temptation and adventure, Paris is an infatuation, Italy is Venice, a feast for the senses. Spain, though, is the Spanish people. Hemingway has felt deeply involved with his people ever since he set foot in their country.... Hemingway felt the tragedy of the Spanish freedom fighters far more deeply than the suffering and sacrifice of any other people under the yoke of Fascism.[15]

Hemingway was not a communist; he was not a socialist either; in fact, he had no political ideology as such; nevertheless, he was outstandingly an anti-Fascist. Almost throughout this part of his life, he kept on moving to and fro between Europe and America, and it was towards the end of the fourth decade of the present century that he got settled in a coastal village near Havana in Cuba. The Leftist revolution that took place in Cuba a few years later unnerved him; he came back to America, in the process losing much of his property and literary material in Cuba itself.

Ernest Hemingway was a literary pilgrim in the real sense of the term. He was profoundly conscious as much of the brutalities and horrors of war as of the various other phenomena afflicting human society. It is this acute awareness of the contemporary human predicament that prompted Hemingway to adopt and develop a code of values that conditioned the course of his own life, the conduct and response of his important characters, and the nature and function of images and symbols in his writings.

II

Although Hemingway started his literary career with the

writing of poems, and later wrote one play, *The Fifth Column*, on the basis of his experiences of the Spanish Civil War, he was basically a prose writer, a writer of fiction. It is true that, by his very temperament, he was perhaps too independent to work steadily under any influence, still war and journalism shaped his life and writings to an extent. 'Journalism and war' says Leo Lania, '...had the greatest effect on his literary development,'[16] and they 'moulded and decided his style, his art, his whole life.'[17] At this point, it is also pertinent to mention that Hemingway did not go to any college or university for higher studies, that his formal education was limited only to the school level, and that he was 'the only representative American author who had never been to a University.'[18] It is in the light of these basic considerations that we have to trace the nature and magnitude of influences under which Hemingway did labour at different points in his literary career.

Since Hemingway belonged to a rather prosperous family of Oak Park, he cannot be said to have suffered an unhappy childhood, and yet his childhood was not quite happy, first because he found himself ill at ease in the genteel but conservative Oak Park society with its heritage of New England Puritanism, and secondly because he could not help getting bruised by the tension straining the relationship between his father and mother. While Hemingway's physician father was interested in adventures and outdoor activities, in hunting, swimming and fishing, his mother had her own commitment to and fascination for religion and music, and these two rivals tried to place their first male child under his or her own tutelage. Hemingway had certainly nothing to do with religion and had very little interest in the church choir. And though he was drawn, if at all, towards his father, being precocious, a craving for independence was generated within him right from his early days. The obvious result was that while, on the one hand, he maintained his lure for adventures, on the other, he got more and more inclined towards literature.

Hemingway's stay at the Oak Park High School was quite

significant and productive, because, besides getting formally initiated into the world of literature, of long narrative poems, myths and novels that formed part of the curriculum, he received a rigorous training in literary composition under the expert supervision of two of his teachers, Miss Gibbs and Miss Dixon. Hemingway, thus, could form his first taste for style at this very time of his life. The poems he wrote during his school-days clearly betray Kipling's influence; in them, he adopts the rhythm of Kipling's ballads, and tries to infuse into them the verve, the unsentimental hardness and virility of Kipling's verse. It is really interesting to find that in respect of his school journalism, he made serious efforts to imitate Ring Lardner, an eminent columnist of the Chicago *Tribune* who was indeed a journalistic sensation at Oak Park and who was also Hemingway's model journalist.

It was chiefly because of Hemingway's growing impatience with formal education and his craving for independence in life that he took to journalism and joined the Kansas City *Star* as a reporter. And it was really fortunate for him as the *Star* reporter that he was greatly influenced by two of his senior colleagues, C.G. Wellington and Lionel Calhoun Moise, who not only guided him in preparing useful and interesting reports for the journal but also encouraged him to undertake literary activities in a purposeful and effective manner. Hemingway's literary pilgrimage, in a way, starts with his joining the Kansas City *Star,* for it was from Kansas that he went to Italy to join the war there, got severely injured, but luckily survived the grievous injuries he had received from his involvement in the trench warfare. Italy provided him with the much sought-after opportunity to encounter war, and this first experience of war generated in Hemingway a kind of moral and spiritual awakening that guided him nearly all through his life. His return to Toronto as a journalist gave a definite shape to his development as a writer and though his journalistic stint in Chicago was rather a tame and unpleasant affair, it was there that he came in touch with Sherwood Anderson.

Hemingway did indeed have several things in common with Anderson: he shared with Anderson an insistence on sex as a basic human drive; like Anderson, he too was drawn to a study of youth and its distress, and they also shared a sense of the importance of emotion and feeling both in life and in art. Hemingway read Anderson's works constantly in Toronto; Anderson was 'a spur, a symbol, as well as a tangible material prop,'[19] and yet as individuals 'they were so fundamentally in competition that they could not remain close for any length of time.'[20] Sherwood Anderson, says Leo Lania, 'had a decisive influence on Hemingway, so decisive that many critics later declared that Hemingway had consciously copied and adopted his style and subject matter, but Anderson denied this allegation in his own memoirs.'[21] In his turn, Anderson says that though it was through his efforts that Hemingway first got published, he goes on to state: 'Anyway it is sure that if others said I had shown Hemingway the way, I myself had never said so. I thought...he had his own gift, which had nothing particularly to do with me.'[22] However, it was with Anderson's direct help and encouragement that Hemingway left for Paris which was to play a crucial role in Hemingway's career as a literary artist.

Hemingway met, among others, Gertrude Stein, Ezra Pound and James Joyce in Paris itself, while he came across Max Beerbohm during one of his travels on the continent. Gertrude Stein was an American novelist whose 'role as discoverer and patroness of struggling artists and poets from Picasso to James Joyce far outshone her literary significance. During the 'twenties her "salon" was a symbol of literary Paris.'[23] Stein told Hemingway that 'writing could be a laborious and exacting process,'[24] that 'journalistic immediacy was not a genuine immediacy,'[25] and that he should stop being 'a newspaper man.'[26] It is indeed very succinctly that Fenton sums up the nature and degree of Hemingway's indebtedness to Gertrude Stein:

> She helped him discover not only what he was seeing, and how to communicate the sight, but what to look for. It was she who explained that he must look at his

> material, and at each new experience, as certain painters.... Cézanne, in particular...looked at their own compositions. His own subsequent dictums on writing are often variations and extensions of what she had either told him or helped him to learn.[27]

Interestingly enough, Hemingway himself acknowledges his gratefulness to Miss Stein with due frankness. Writing to Gertrude Stein in 1924, Hemingway says: 'Writing used to be easy before I met you.'[28] Hemingway had always been willing, in fact, anxious to work hard at his writing, but it was Miss Stein who pointed out to him how to make it profitably hard.

Ezra Pound was one of the first in Paris to recognize Hemingway's great talents. Hemingway and Pound became close friends, and they remained friends until such time as Pound's political views, his anti-Semitic and Fascist leanings, destroyed their friendship. However, apart from Pound's literary judgement and his practical advice, Hemingway 'esteemed the tireless way in which he was always prepared to help aspiring young authors.'[29]

It is difficult to say that Hemingway was influenced by any or all such great writers as Tolstoy, Dostoevsky and Turgenev from Russia, Hawthorne, Melville, Mark Twain and Henry James from America, Henry Fielding, Emily Bronte and James Joyce from England, Stendhal, Flaubert and Maupassant from France, and Thomas Mann from Germany, but it is on record that while compiling a list of books he considered priceless, Hemingway mentioned such works as Tolstoy's *Anna Karenina* and *War and Peace,* Dostoevsky's *The Brothers Karamazov,* all of Turgenev's works, Mark Twain's *Hucklebурry Finn,* Henry James's and Sherwood Anderson's short stories, Emily Bronte's *Wuthering Heights,* Kipling's short stories, Joyce's *Ulysses* and *The Dubliners,* Stendhal's *The Scarlet and the Black,* Flaubert's *Madame Bovary,* Maupassant's *The House of Madame Tellier* and Thomas Mann's *Buddenbrooks.*

The one great non-literary influence on Hemingway was that of William Bolitho, the representative of the Manchaster

Guardian at Lousanne, who, 'like Miss Stein, advised him not to adopt journalism as a career, and who strengthened in Hemingway his knowledgeability, his instinct for being on the inside, and his insistence that one should think for himself.'[30] Hemingway himself ungrudgingly accepts that Bolitho 'taught me to think for myself.'[31]

A number of writers, as we see, might have influenced, either directly or indirectly, Hemingway's mind and art, and similarly a number of events and phenomena, such as World War I, Graeco-Turkish War, Spanish Civil War, World War II and Fascism, might have affected him to an appreciable extent, and yet it is Hemingway's personal grit, his capacity to endure suffering and his commitment to write only about what he has experienced in his own characteristic prose that chiefly determine the nature or quality of his writings.

III

There should be no hestitation in accepting the fact that Hemingway has been a popular writer and that a good deal has been written and is still being written on him, on his narrative art, his characters, his attitude towards life, his prose style and his individual works. It is really interesting to see that while on the one hand, T.S. Eliot views Hemingway's popularity with suspicion and calls it 'largely undeserved,'[32] on the other, D.S.R. Welland maintains that 'the English novel would have developed differently had (Hemingway) not written.'[33] At this point, it would certainly be pertinent to take a workable stock of Hemingway's reputation as a writer of fiction.

In his essay on *The Sun Also Rises* James T. Farrell, while conceding some ground to Hemingway, calls him only 'a writer of limited vision.' He says:

> Hemingway is a writer of limited vision, one who has no broad and fertile perspective of life. Younger writers were influenced — even seduced — by his moods; and they could grasp from him a sense of the great possibilities to be discovered in the true and simple treatment of common subject matter and in the use of ordinary speech.

> But once they had learned these lessons, they could gain a little more from Hemingway.[34]

Farrell accepts Hemingway's use of ordinary speech rather with a feeling of satisfaction, but he wonders if Hemingway did really have any evolved and articulate attitude towards the problems plaguing mankind.

However, Carlos Baker has to say something different about Hemingway. He comments:

> The basis of Hemingway's continuing power, and the real backbone of his eminence, is in practical esthetics. "Pure" or theoretical esthetics, of that special bloodless order which can argue to all hours without a glance at concentrations, holds little interest for an artist of so pragmatic and empirical a cast of mind. One might even doubt that theoretical esthetics is of real interest to any genuine artist, unless in his alter ego he happens also to be a philosophical critic. If that is true, his artistic life is always in some danger, as Hemingway's is not. In esthetics as in his personal philosophy, he has labored hard to stay free of the wrong kind of illusion, and out from under the control of any cut-and dried system, always trying instead to keep his eye trained on the thing in itself and the effect of the thing in himself.[35]

Carlos Baker calls Hemingway an artist with a pragmatic and empirical cast of mind, and states that, whether in the field of aesthetics or in that of philosophy, he did always try to keep himself away from illusions. Similarly, Baker takes pains to argue that Hemingway's artistic belief is so very clear and outstanding. He says:

> As he (Hemingway) worked through the complexities of his task, Hemingway was sustained by a belief he had long held to: the job of the artist is not to judge but to understand. No matter how hard it may be to believe it in our political age, there is such a thing as the artistic 'neutrality' of one who puts humanity above politics and art above propaganda.[36]

Baker maintains that Hemingway was a votary of artistic neutrality, that he was neither a political writer nor a propagandist, and that he did put humanity above politics and art above propaganda.

E.M. Halliday is of the view that in spite of Hemingway's dexterous use of irony and symbolism in his works, he remains only a realist and that, in fact, symbolism and irony protect and bring into sharper relief his commitment to realism. Halliday observes:

> Taken at face value the denomination 'symbolist' has meanings in the common language of criticism that are quite inapplicable to him (Hemingway). But beyond this, Hemingway uses symbolism...with a severe restraint that in his good work always staunchly protects his realism. So likewise does he use irony. It is the ambiguity of life itself that Hemingway has sought to render, and if irony has served him peculiarly well it is because he sees life as inescapably ironic. But if we must classify him let us do him justice: with all his skilful use of artistic ambiguity, he remains the great *realist* of twentieth century American fiction.[37]

And here is Leo Lania who informs us that Hemingway did never belong to 'any of the recognised modern literary schools'[38] and that 'in the age of expressionism he was an impressionist, almost neo-classic in his precise presentation of detail, his respect for form and discipline, his desire for perfection, the exact phrase, the right word.'[39]

As we go through a substantial part of the corpus of Hemingway criticism, we find ourselves face-to-face with an engaging kind of controversy going on as to the real nature of the theme running through his fictional writings. While on the one hand it is said that what we get in Hemingway is nothing serious but only fun, on the other, it is maintained that what he seeks to offer us is a tragic vision of life that has its own value and profundity. Philip Young expresses the view that Hemingway is neither serious-minded nor profound and that, at best, he is only a prophet of doom. It is in this very connection that, while comparing *The Waste Land* with *The Sun Also Rises* and *A Farewell to Arms*, he says:

> In the poem a message of salvation comes out of the life-giving rain which falls on western civilization. In Hemingway's wasteland there is fun, but there is no hope. No rain falls on Europe this time, and when it does fall, in *A Farewell to Arms*, it brings not life but death.[40]

More or less almost in a similar vein, John Killinger too is not at all inclined to agree with those who look upon Hemingway as a philosophical novelist in general or as an existentialist in particular. He states:

> Properly speaking, Hemingway is not an existentialist, for there has been no known liaison between him and the existentialists, either personally or intellectually, and neither has ever formally recognised a kinship to the other.... But it is more likely that the similarities in their world-views are due not to collaboration, but to living in the same milieu....[41]

Killinger is of the opinion that if at all there are points of similarity between Hemingway on the one hand and the existentialists on the other, it is not really because of the similarities in their attitudes but because of their belonging to a similar ethos or set of experiences.

In his essay on *A Farewell to Arms entitled* 'The Mountain and the Plain,' Carlos Baker takes the stand that Hemingway is one of the foremost tragic writers in the field of twentieth-century fiction. He observes:

> The appearance of *A Farewell to Arms* in book form on September 27, 1929, marked the inception of Hemingway's still lengthening career as one of the very few great tragic writers in twentieth-century fiction. His next book, *Death in the Afternoon*, furthered his exploration into the esthetics of tragedy. Through the 1930's he continued at intervals to wrestle with the problem. *To Have and Have Not* (though with limited success) examined the tragic implications of social and political decay. *For Whom the Bell Tolls* attacked a similar problem on an epic and international scale.[42]

Baker says that with the publication of *A Farewell to Arms* in 1929, Hemingway started exploring the tragic implications of the political, moral and cultural decay in the present age and that he has carried on this exploration in the books that were written subsequently. In a way, Baker resists the idea of considering Hemingway as just an easy-going story-teller interested chiefly in sex and crime and violence and the concomitant phenomena. As we find Baker, he attributes a level and degree of seriousness to Hemingway that is generally true of a genuine intellectual and thinker.

In his essay captioned 'The Death of Love in *The Sun Also Rises*' among other things, Mark Spilka observes that one of Hemingway's prime concerns as a writer of fiction is love, or to be sure, the death of love in the post-First World War world. He points out:

> One of the most persistent themes of the twenties was the death of love in World War I. All the major writers recorded it, often in piecemeal fashion as a part of the larger post-war scene; but only Hemingway seems to have caught it whole and delivered it in lasting fictional form. His intellectual grasp of the theme might account for this. Where D.H. Lawrence settles for the shock of war on the Phallic Consciousness, or where Eliot presents assorted glimpses of sterility, Hemingway seems to design an extensive parable.[43]

Spilka expresses the view that in his fictional works, quite a few of which are in the nature of parables, Hemingway deals with the issue of death of love in the modern times in a manner different from that of Lawrence or Eliot. In his turn, Lionel Trilling too refers to the very element, the death of love, as he finds it patterened in Hemingway's fictions. He comments:

> ...one feels of love in the Hemingway novels that it can exist at all only because circumstances so surely doom it. We do not have to venture very deep into unexpressed meanings to find a connection between Hemingway's social myth and the pattern of his love stories...in both there is a desperation which makes a quick grab for simple perfection. This desperation makes understandable the compulsive turning to courage as the saving and

> solving virtue. The whole complex of attitude is...a way of responding to the imminent idea of death.[44]

Trilling explains Hemingway's credo of courage in terms of his feeling of desperation in a world where love is doomed.

In his very illuminating essay entitled 'Hemingway: The Matador and the Crucified,' Melvin Backman speaks of two dominant motifs running through Hemingway's writings, the one being that of the matador, while the other being that of the crucified. He says:

> Running through Ernest Hemingway's work from *In Our Time* to *The Old Man and the Sea* are two dominant motifs — the matador and the crucified. The matador represents a great force held in check, releasing itself proudly in a controlled yet violent administering of death. The crucified stands for the taking of pain, even unto death, with all of one's courage and endurance so that it becomes a thing of poignancy and nobility. Although it was not until *The Old Man and the Sea* that Hemingway achieved a perfect blending of his two themes, the continual tension and interplay between those forces represented by the matador and the crucified create a pattern in the Hemingway canon against which the individual works of fiction may be profitably studied.[45]

According to Backman, it is the tension between these two forces signified by the matador and the crucified that lends a striking kind of sublimity to Hemingway's fiction and in the light of which his individual works have to be justifiably interpreted. In fact, Backman invests Hemingway's fictional works with a religious grandeor of sorts and it is, precisely speaking, in terms of religion that Joseph Waldmeir seeks to view Hemingway's novels. Waldmeir observes:

> Hemingway did not turn religious to write *The Old Man and the Sea*. He has always been religious, though his religion is not of orthodox, organized variety. He celebrates, he has always celebrated, the Religion of Man; *The Old Man and the Sea* merely celebrates it more forcefully and convincingly than any previous Hemingway work. It is the final step in the celebration.

> It is the book which, on the one hand, elevates the philosophy to a religion by the use of allegory, and on the other, by being an allegory of the total body of his work, enables us to see that work finally from the point of view of religion.[46]

It is almost universally known that Hemingway was not a religious writer, or that he did not believe in a formal, dogmatic, or institutionalised kind of religion. He was not at all a man of religion in the sense Graham Greene is; even so, he was religious in the sense that he believed in and practised what may be called the Religion of Man. Naturally enough, it would be implausible to look upon Hemingway also as a moralist in a specific sense, as one who did have his own scale and view of ethical considerations in a world ravaged by war, unprecedented physical destruction and loss of traditional values. In this connection Clinton S. Burhans, Jr. comments:

> ...Hemingway is a moralist; heir, like his world, to the destruction by science and empiricism of nineteenth-century value assumptions and the principle underlying them...that intellectual moral abstractions possess supersensual existence. Turning from the resulting nihilism, he goes to experience in the actual world of hostility, violence, and destruction to find in the world which destroyed the old values a basis for new ones...and it is precisely here...that Hemingway is a significant moralist.[47]

Burhans asserts that Hemingway was a moralist, that he was not a nihilist who turned away from or rejected all values, and that he was a moralist, not in an intellectual or abstract sense, but in a significant or effective sense, in a sense that underscores the practical values of toughness and resistance, of confrontation and action in a world shorn of all established values.

The Hemingway scholars and critics have expressed their views not only in respect of the theme, the basic stuff, or the nature of his novels but also with regard to his style, for Hemingway's prose style has a singular identity, a special charm and appeal of its own. It is usually said that Hemingway's is a sparse, uniform and monotonous kind of prose style, replete with such connectives as 'but' and 'and;' however, the truth is that the simplicity of his prose generates its own beauty as well as its own effectiveness. In this context Joseph Warren Beach says:

> The sentiment is not wanting in Hemingway. But he finds that he can give more point to his sentiment if he does not dress it out in fine language. And all the more so because this method requires more skill than that which depends on fine language for making its point. It requires that the facts shall be so rightly ordered that they will speak for themselves. This is a challenge to the serious artist. The undiscriminating reader may miss the intention and confuse this work with pulp. But if the thing is done with skill and subtlety, the discriminating reader will not long miss it; and he will receive a pleasure proportioned to the difficulty of the undertaking.[48]

Beach is clearly of the view that the writing of the kind of Hemingway's prose may look easy, but it requires the sort of skill and subtlety which only the discriminating reader can appreciate. In his turn, Mark Schorer undertakes an incisive analysis of Hemingway's prose from a different position, and says that while in the beginning his prose was qualified by a tension between subject-matter and style, later it underwent a change and came to acquire an altered character. Schorer comments:

> What was for long the sign of Ernest Hemingway's work..the curious tension between subject matter and style, between the themes of violence and the perfectly controlled prose...has gone. Hemingway was extraordinary among modern prose writers for exactly this reason that he pressed his style into the service of his subject matter in a rather special way: the style was immediate representation of the moral attitude of the author toward his material, it objectified the author's values and thus in itself was comment in writing otherwise unhampered by comment. When, however, the subject matter began to change...from violent experience itself to the expressed evaluation of violence...the manner began to change.[49]

Schorer is of the view that the change in the nature of Hemingway's prose has been one from a 'neutral' kind of prose to evaluative prose, from understanding to judgement, from a thing in itself to a search for things. However, it is something really important to note that not an inconsiderable part of Hemingway's greatness as a writer rests on the quality or nature of his prose. In fact, as E.M. Halliday points out, Hemingway is so gifted a writer that, without being obstrusive, his prose is as much capable of describing objective action as of revealing the subjective states of mind. Halliday says:

> Hemingway, choosing occasions where objective action and perception have come virtually to a standstill, uses the interior monologue in a manner which maintains all three realistic features of epistemological polarity, naturalistic probability, and immediacy. He was thus able to exploit fully the advantages offered by the first-person method..., while at the same time avoiding the dangers to realism peculiar to that method when it undertakes the exposition of subjective states.[50]

Halliday maintains that Hemingway is a highly successful narrative artist largely, if not chiefly, because of the balance or poise he maintains, through the modulations of his prose, between the demands of the third-person account and the compulsions or constraints of the first-person narrative style.

From Hemingway's prose style and narrative art to his characters is a logical shift in perspective. There is indeed a lot of controversy about the quality, level, or status of his character. D.S. Savage comes out with the opinion that Hemingway's characters are creatures 'without religion, politics, culture or history,'[51] and his novels are without any 'coherently developing pattern.'[52] At his own end, John Atkins is of the view that the change in Hemingway's portrayal of character is one from 'Natural Man to Political Man and back to Natural Man again.'[53] And about the heroines or principal female characters in Hemingway's novels, Carlos Baker says:

> ...all of Hemingway's heroines, like all of his heroes, are placed in a specialised kind of accelerated world. We do not see them puttering in their kitchens, but only dreaming of that as a desirable possibility. They are never

> presented as harassed mothers; their orientation tends to be, in this connection, premarital. Wars and revolutions, the inevitable enemies of peace and domesticity, set them adrift or destroy their lives. Yet they contrive to embody the image of home, the idea if not the actuality of the married state, and where they are, whatever the outward threats, home is.[54]

Baker is rightly of the view that Hemingway's principal female characters have hardly anything to do with domesticity or with the peace and security of a settled married life; and it is also true that his principal male characters, with no foundation whatsoever under their feet, have to conduct themselves through the violence, destruction and instability of a world ravaged by war. Perhaps the only resource they are left with is their own grit, their determination to accept and face the contingency of all-engulfing threats.

IV

As we have seen in the preceding pages, Ernest Hemingway is remembered both as a writer and legend, for, more than anybody else's, in his case the two are nearly inseparable from each other. Hemingway was indeed a prolific writer, and even though he was not very much interested in formal education, he had started writing and contributing to journals while he was just a seventeen-year old boy and a student at the Oak Park school. It is true that, like his father, he too did have a great passion for sports and outdoor activities, and yet by virtue of his precocity he had decided rather early in his life to take to writing as a vocation, and, towards this end, made sustained efforts to learn as much from the world of letters as from his direct encounter with life. His career as a journalist, spread over a large span of time, that took him to various important places in America and Europe, his defiant and persistent participation in wars and revolutions, his close association with the celebrated literary circle of Paris, his anti-Fascist stance, his first-hand experience of human suffering and of the loss of established values in a world ravaged by wars, and his penchant for recording his impressions and experiences in the form of fictional narrative—all these drove Hemingway into adopting a course that helped him in shaping himself as a writer of fiction. It is no wonder, therefore, that he gave us, besides others, such great fictional works as *The Sun Also Rises, A Farewell to Arms, For Whom the Bell Tolls* and *The Old Man and the Sea.*

It may not be very profitable to discuss at length the nature and magnitude of influence that various people, situations and phenomena might have exerted upon Hemingway, for he was the one great American writer who belonged to no acknowledged school or tradition of fiction. And still, as we have said earlier, we cannot do, in this context, without referring, in the first instance, to Hemingway's adverse reaction to the rather conservative and puritanical ambience of Oak Park, to his sense of dilemma over the war of nerves that went on and on between his father and his mother and his predilection for his father in respect of the latter's passion for fishing, swimming and hunting, to the articulate and wholesome training Hemingway received at the hands of two of his Oak Park School teachers, Miss Gibbs and Miss Dixon, and to the inspiration he imbibed, even as a boy, from Rudyard Kipling and Ring Lardner. Secondly, as a journalist, working with the Kansas City *Star,* he was greatly influenced by C.G. Wellington and Lionel Calhoun Moise, who persistently guided him in the art of writing and encouraged him to keep on improving his composition. Yet another journalist who inspired him considerably was William Bolitho Ryall for he 'strengthened in Hemingway his knowlegeability, his instinct for being on the inside, and his insistence that one should think for himself.'[55] Thirdly, if Hemingway was not happy during his stay in Chicago for a brief journalistic stint there on account of what he viewed as American commercialism and American insensitivity to human suffering, he was not close to Sherwood Anderson either. And yet, as we have pointed out earlier, in a certain way Anderson did influence Hemingway. Fourthly, during his stay in Paris, Hemingway learnt a good deal, among others, from Gertrude Stein and Ezra Pound who advised him to take up his literary pursuits seriously, precisely as a matter of hard concentration, and, as a first step towards this, to give up journalism. And, finally, it was Hemingway's experiences and impressions of wars and revolutions, of World War I, Graeco-Turkish War, Spanish Civil War and World War II, that affected him to a substantial degree.

Nevertheless, Hemingway was perhaps too fiercely independent a writer to accept any influence or influences completely or as such, and naturally we have to consider him as a writer of fiction in his own right.

Ernest Hemingway has been read and is still being read widely, and expectedly enough, a lot has been written on his mind and art, on the theme, the basic stuff of his writings, on his writing technique, on the ambiguity, irony and symbolism in his fiction, on his prose style, and on his characters. In this connection we have recorded and analysed what T.S. Eliot, Lionel Trilling, D.S. Savage, John Atkins, Joseph Warren Beach, Mark Schorer, Mark Spilka, Carlos Baker, Leo Lania, Philip Young, Charles A. Fenton, D.S.R. Welland, James T. Farell, E.M. Halliday, John Killinger, Melvin Backman, Joseph Waldmeir and Clinton S. Burhans, Jr. have to say on the issues or problems in question. It is not at all difficult to see that Hemingway's reputation does register a sharp curve either upward or downward, and that while quite a few scholars and critics look upon his fictional writings as meaningful, profound and well-executed literary exercises, there are others who find him only cheap, superficial, and rather addicted to sensationalism. What is obviously required is a patient, thorough and balanced estimate of Hemingway as a writer of fiction.

REFERENCES

1. L. Lania, *Hemingway: A Pictorial Biography* (New York, 1961), 5.
2. Two of Hemingway's novels, *Islands in the Stream* and *The Garden of Eden* were published posthumously in 1970 and 1986 respectively.
3. Charles A. Fenton, *The Apprenticeship of Ernest Hemingway* (New York, 1954), 13.
4. Fenton 13.

5. Charles A. Fenton, *The Apprenticeship of Ernest Hemingway* (New York, 1954), 17.
6. Fenton 17.
7. *Kansas City Times,* Nov. 26, 1940, 1.
8. Charles A. Fenton, *The Apprenticeship of Ernest Hemingway* (New York, 1954), 37-38.
9. Ernest Hemingway, *Green Hills of Africa* (New York, 1935), 70.
10. Ernest Hemingway, 'Introduction:' *Men at War* (New York, 1942), XVI.
11. Charles A. Fenton, *The Apprenticeship of Ernest Hemingway* (New York, 1954), 81.
12. Fenton 81.
13. H.M. Jones & Walter B. Rideout (eds.), *Letters of Sherwood Anderson* (New York, 1953), 82-83.
14. Harvey Breit, 'Talk with Mr. Hemingway,' *New York Times Book Review,* lv (Sept. 17, 1950), 14.
15. L. Lania, *Hemingway: A Pictorial Biography* (New York, 1961), 101-2.
16. Lania, *Hemingway: A Pictorial Biography* (New York, 1961), 27.
17. Lania, Hemingway 27.
18. Lania, Hemingway 27.
19. Charles A. Fenton, *The Apprenticeship of Ernest Hemingway* (New York, 1954), 105.
20. Fenton 105.
21. Lania, *Hemingway: A Pictorial Biography* (New York, 1961), 40.
22. Sherwood Anderson, *Sherwood Anderson's Memoirs* (New York, 1942), 474-75.
23. Lania, *Hemingway: A Pictorial Biography* (New York, 1961), 44.
24. Charles A. Fenton, *The Apprenticeship of Ernest Hemingway* (New York, 1954), 147.
25. Fenton 158.
26. Fenton 159.
27. Fenton 154.
28. D. Gallup (ed.), *The Flowers of Friendship: Letters Written to Gertrude Stein* (Chicago, 1953), 165.
29. L. Lania, *Hemingway: A Pictorial Biography* (New York, 1961), 49.
30. Charles A. Fenton, *The Apprenticeship of Ernest Hemingway* (New York, 1954), 195.

31. Walter Duranty, *I Write as I Please* (London, 1935), 169.
32. Roger Assilineau (ed.), *The Literary Reputation of Hemingway in Europe* (New York, 1965), 20.
33. Roger Assilineau 33.
34. James T. Farrell, *The League of Frightened Philistines* (New York, 1945), 22-23.
35. Carlos Baker, *Hemingway: The Writer as Artist* (Princeton, 1956), 58.
36. Baker 240.
37. E.M. Halliday, 'Hemingway's Ambiguity: Symbolism and Irony,' *American Literature,* xxvii (March, 1956), 22.
38. L. Lania, *Hemingway: A Pictorial Biography* (New York, 1961), 6.
39. Lania 7.
40. Philip Young, *Ernest Hemingway* (New York, 1952), 60.
41. Johh Killinger, *Hemingway and the Dead Gods: A Study in Existentialism* (Kentucky, 1960), vii.
42. Carlos Baker, *Hemingway: The Writer as Artist* (Princeton, 1956), 98.
43. Charles Shapiro (ed.), *Twelve Original Essays on Great American Novels* (Detroit, 1958), 238-39.
44. Philip Rahv and William Philip (eds.), *The Partisan Reader* (New York, 1946), 643-44.
45. C. Baker (ed.), *Hemingway and His Critics: An International Anthology* (New York, 1961), 245.
46. J. Waldmeir, Confiteor Hominem: Ernest Hemingway's Religion of Man,' Papers of the Michigan Academy of Science, Arts, and Letters xlii (Ann Arbor : Michigan, 1957), 356.
47. C.S. Burhans, Jr., '*The Old Man and the Sea* Hemingway's Tragic Vision of Man,' *American Literature* (Jan., 1960), xxxi, 454.
48. J.W. Beach, *American Fiction 1920-1924* (New York, 1941), 111.
49. M. Schorer, 'The Background of a Style', *Kenyon Review,* iii (Winter, 1941), 101.
50. E.M. Halliday, 'Hemingway's Narrative Perspective,' *Sewanee Review,* 1x (Spring, 1952), 209.
51. D.S. Savage, *The Withered Branch* (London, 1950), 27.
52. Savage 27-28.
53. J. Atkins, *The Art of Ernest Hemingway* (London, 1952), 46.
54. C. Baker, *Hemingway: The Writer as Artist* (Princeton, 1956), 113-14.
55. Charles A. Fenton, *The Apprenticeship of Ernest Hemingway* (New York, 1954), 195.

2

The Sun Also Rises

ERNEST HEMINGWAY'S first novel, *The Sun Also Rises,* was published in 1926, and, as we go through the book, it becomes unmistakably clear to us that the period of time that this book covers in respect of action is just one year, that is, 1925. In the post-First World War era, the world was rather returning to normalcy and the European economy was gradually picking up its desired tempo. It is a period of disarmament and peace treaties, of conferences on progress and co-operation, and indeed of growing stability. It was an era of guarded hope and happiness, for the threat of war, insurgency, revolution, or counter-revolution had nearly receded. Moreover, it was an era in which America had emerged as a powerful country, a country enjoying not merely political authority but also great industrial progress and economic boom. Nevertheless, what we find in *The Sun Also Rises,* or for that matter in Hemingway's other novels too, is an air of disenchantment, a climate of ennui or boredom, an atmosphere of morbidity, depression or futility that goes counter to the general physical condition of Europe. Naturally enough, in his essay on *The Sun Also Rises,* James T. Farrell comments: 'It may seem paradoxical that in such a period a novel of war disillusionment, nihilistic in outlook, should have become an international success.'[1] However, it is not at all difficult to explain this seeming paradox or contradiction if we examine the whole thing in the right perspective.

Perhaps all the people who had actually participated in war, or had been its victims in one way or another, were, quite understandably, disenchanted with life because of its horrors and brutalities. However, far more than physical injury, war had caused a kind of psychological crisis and moral degradation on account of which the post-war period was one of delicate and difficult adjustment with the realities of life. 'Hemingway,' as Philip Young puts it, 'had deeply felt and understood what was in the wind.'[2] Jacob or Jake Barnes, the hero of *The Sun Also Rises,* has been rendered impotent on account of the injuries inflicted on him during the war, but, more or less, he has reconciled himself to the conditions of his life. As Barnes is moving about with Georgette, a prostitute, he has picked up accidently, he asks her:

> 'What's the matter? You sick?'
>
> 'Yes.'
>
> 'Everybody's sick. I'm sick, too.'[3]

According to Farrell, 'A re-examination of the character of disillusionment portrayed in *The Sun Also Rises* suggests that this mood had become a way of feeling and acting; in fact, a social habit.'[4] This mood of sickness or disenchantment with life, not unnaturally, prompted people to be rather nihilistic in their attitude and discard every form of middle-class respectability. And, not unexpectedly, Hemingway tries to express this mood through escapades, through a search for new sensations, through acts of calculated bravado, through drinking, fishing, bull-fighting and sexual exploits, through regular visits to clubs, cafés, hotels and restaurants. One of the titles of the present novel, *Fiesta,* is, as such, utterly significant.

In *The Sun Also Rises,* written in the first person, almost all the characters, except for Robert Cohn, look alike, are alike, and form a special group of their own. In several of its early editions, *The Sun Also Rises* had on its title page Gertrude Stein's famous statement: 'You are all a lost generation.' And, as Mark Spilka observes, in a broader sense, these characters are 'all disaffiliates, all men and women who have cut themselves off from conventional society and who have made Paris their permanent playground.'[5]

II

The first striking image that we come across in *The Sun Also Rises* is that of emptiness, an image that is rendered in various ways and forms and which is very much in consonance with the general mood or temper of the novel. In Chapter 6 of the present novel, Hemingway gives us a picture of empty barges being towed down the current, and it is significant that Jake Barnes watches their movement on the Seine:

> Brett had not been in the bar either, and so I looked for her upstairs on my way out, and took a taxi for the Café Select. Crossing the Seine I saw a string of barges being towed empty down the current, riding high, the bargemen at the sweeps as they came towards the bridge.[6]

And later in the same chapter, Jake Barnes goes to a café which has very few people inside it and where Jake notices a pile of empty saucers lying on a table before Harvey Stone:

> No matter what café in Montparnasse you ask a taxi-driver to bring you to from the right bank of the river, they always take you to the Rotonde. Ten years from now it will probably be the Dome. It was near enough, anyway. I walked past the sad tables of the Rotonde to the Select. There were a few people inside at the bar, and outside, alone, sat Harvey Stone. He had a pile of saucers in front of him....[7]

This feeling of emptiness is indeed a pervading presence in *The Sun Also Rises.*

It is indeed remarkable to see that even while the Spanish town of Pamplona is getting ready for the fiesta and the place is bracing itself up for the occasion, Hemingway speaks of the empty stands of the amphitheatre surrounding the bull-ring. He says: 'Standing at the edge of the smooth rolled sand you could look up in the empty stands and see old women sweeping out the boxes.'[8] Similarly, after the fiesta is over, as Jake Barnes, Bill Gorton and Mike Campbell are about to leave for Pamplona, Jake looks at the empty town square which, only a day earlier, was bristling with activity and looking colourful and resplendent in the glow of festive celebrations:

> The fiesta was finished. I woke about nine o'clock, had a bath, dressed, and went downstairs. The square was empty and there were no people on the streets. A few children were picking up rocket-sticks in the square. The cafés were just opening and the waiters were carrying out the comfortable wicker chairs and arranging them around the marble-topped tables in the shade of the arcade. They were sweeping the streets and sprinkling them with a hose.[9]

And, likewise, as Bill Gorton is leaving Bayonne for Paris by train, Jake watches the empty rail-tracks that do seem to hold out to him a peculiar kind of significance:

> He went in through the gate to the train. The porter went ahead with the bags. I watched the train pull out. Bill was at one of the windows. The window passed, the rest of the train passed, and the tracks were empty.[10]

The empty stands, the empty square and the empty rail-tracks—they are all of a piece, suggesting the futility and meaninglessness of human life.

It is in a similar vein that, once again, we get an image of empty coffee-glasses and cognac-glasses in Chapter 16 of the present novel:

> He sat down and looked at her across the table. I went out. The hard-eyed people at the bull-fighter table watched me go. It was not pleasant. When I came back and looked in the café, twenty minutes later, Brett and Pedro Romero were gone. The coffee-glasses and the three empty cognac-glasses were on the table. A waiter came with a cloth and picked up the glasses and mopped off the table.[11]

Brett Ashley and the bull-fighter, Pedro Romero, are steadily moving closer and closer to each other. For Jake Barnes, this is surely an interesting development, since he knows that this growing closeness is as much incompatible as any such proximity between listlessness and life, between experience and sheer youthfulness.

However, these images of emptiness, signifying loss, decay

or separation, are generally followed by the images of cleansing, mopping up or sweeping, and they have their own bearing as much on the theme of the novel as on the given situations and the nature or attitude of individual characters.

Quite a few of the other images that we get in *The Sun Also Rises* relate chiefly to Robert Cohn and bring out the essential nature of his character. Cohn is a Jew 'a member, through his father, of one of the richest Jewish family in New York, and through his mother of one of the oldest'[12] and was 'once middleweight boxing champion of Princeton.'[13] He has been a football player, a tennis player, a bridge player, and, besides, a bit of a novelist too, for, as the author says, he 'wrote a novel...although it was a very poor novel.'[14] However, what is really most relevant about him is that though he moves in the company of Jake Barnes, Brett Ashley and others in Paris as well as in Spain, really speaking, he is not one of them. His immaturity, his lack of perceptiveness, his wayward youthfulness and his sickening ways of behaviour are brought into sharp focus only to be contradistinguished from the manners and mannerisms of the other major characters of this novel. The very fact that Hemingway speaks of him in terms of his 'suitcase with (the) football things in it,'[15] his 'polo shirt'[16] and his 'boxing fits and crying'[17] suggests that here is a character who is not at all sure of himself and who, as such, canot make a proper assessment of the prevailing situation. He claims to be ardently in love with Brett Ashley; he looks at her as 'his compatriot must have looked when he saw the promised land,'[18] and yet the fact of the matter is that he has 'never been in love in his life.'[19] He is a bit of an imposter; even so, when he learns from Jake Barnes that Brett Ashley has gone off with the bull-fighter, Pedro Romero, he flies into a rage and hits him hard:

> I swung at him and he ducked. I saw his face duck sideways in the light. He hit me and I sat down on the pavement. As I started to get on my feet he hit me twice. I went down backwards under a table. I tried to get up and felt I did not have any legs. I felt I must get on my feet and try and hit him. Mike helped me up. Someone

> poured a carafe of water on my head. Mike had an arm around me and I found I was sitting on a chair. Mike was pulling at my ears.
> 'I say, you were cold.' Mike said.
> 'Where the hell were you?'
> 'Oh, I was around.'
> 'You didn't want to mix in it?'
> 'He knocked Mike down, too,' Edna said.
> 'He didn't knock me out'
> Mike said. 'I just lay there.'
> 'Does this happen every night at your fiestas?' Edna asked.
> 'Wasn't that Mr. Cohn?'[20]

Robert Cohn's polo shirt and his phantom suitcase, observes Mark Spilka in his essay entitled 'The Death of Love in *The Sun Also Rises*,' 'remind us (immediately) of one of those dreamlike fantasies by the Czech genius Franz Kafka, in which trunks and youthful clothes are symbols of arrested development.'[21] In the course of one of his authorial comments, Hemingway himself says that there is 'a funny short of undergraduate quality'[22] about Cohn, and Harvey Stone describes Cohn's case as one of 'arrested development.'[23]

Robert Cohn is an odd character, almost an absurd character, and yet he occupies a key position in the novel. He is, as Mark Spilka puts it, 'the last chivalric hero, the last defender of an outworn faith, and his function is to illustrate its present folly—to show us, through the absurdity of his behaviour, that romantic love is dead, that one of the great guiding codes of the past no longer operates.'[24]

If Jake Barnes and his friends are by and large dissillusioned people, rootless and shaky and rather lost; and if Robert Cohn is a false romantic hero, then Pedro Romero is a character who is rooted in the Spanish tradition and soil. He is a simple and unassuming person: there is, as the novelist himself says, 'nothing conceited or braggartly about him,'[25] and though only nineteen years old, he does have his own sense of self-confidence and dignity to keep him utterly unruffled. He is a trained and accomplished bull-fighter with a handsome face and smokes only cigars because they form 'part of his system of authority'[26] and make him 'seem older.'[27] He takes on Brett Ashley as slowly and as surely as he takes on bulls inside the ring, and even though he is thrashed repeatedly by Robert Cohn, he remains undefeated both physically and spiritually. Pedro Romero stands for virility, and personifies everything good that would survive the failure of Jake Barnes and his associates.

As we go through *The Sun Also Rises,* we find that there are certain images in the novel, the figurative as well as the descriptive image, that present to us an integrated picture of happiness, growth and fruitfulness. The spirit of freedom and gaiety that is associated with 'fishing' in the Irati river at Burguete in Spain is the first case in point:

> We stayed five days at Burguete and had good fishing. The nights were cold and the days were hot, and there was always a breeze even in the heat of the day. It was hot enough so that it felt good to wade in a cold stream, and the sun dried you when you came out and sat on the bank. We found a stream with a pool deep enough to swim in. In the evenings we played three-handed bridge with an Englishman named Harris, who had walked over from Saint Jean Pied de Port and was stopping at the inn for the fishing. He was very pleasant and went with us twice to the Irati river.[28]

Similarly, the way Hemingway describes the ritualistic bull-fight and the fiesta makes us aware of the fact that in spite of all depression and despair and morbidity, life does have a built-in mechanism of its own to assert and reassert itself over adverse situations:

> The fiesta was really started. It kept up day and night for seven days. The dancing kept up, the drinking kept up, the noise went on. The things that happened could only have happened during a fiesta. Everything became quite unreal finally and it seemed as though nothing could have any consequences. It seemed out of place to think of

> consequences during the fiesta. All during the fiesta you had the feeling, even when it was quiet, that you had to shout any remark to make it heard. It was the same feeling about any action. It was a fiesta and it went on for seven days.[29]

It is important to note that it is only during the fiesta that we come across happy interludes in the novel; before and after the fiesta it is all emptiness.

It is, more or less, in a similar vein that we encounter the goat image in Chapter 12 of the present novel. Significantly enough, this image is introduced immediately after the description of hard wind blowing and roofs cracking in a foul and troublesome weather. Jake is delighted to see a goat hopping up and down on a cart in the morning following the stormy night:

> When I woke in the morning I went to the window and looked out. It had cleared and there were no clouds on the mountains. Outside under the window were some carts and an old diligence, the wood of the roof cracked and split by the weather. It must have been left from the days before the motor-buses. A goat hopped up on one of the carts and then to the roof of the diligence. He jerked his head at the other goats below and when I waved at him he bounded down.[30]

The goat, it is so very clear to us, stands for energy and agility, for hope and joy. And, quite understandably, it is in order to give us a picture of growth and fulfilment that, in the following passage, Hemingway describes the Burguete landscape, as the tourists view it:

> We walked on the road between the thick trunks of the old beeches and the sunlight came through the leaves in light patches on the grass. The trees were big, and the foliage was thick but it was not gloomy. There was no undergrowth, only the smooth grass, very green and fresh, and the big grey trees well spaced as though it were a park.... There were wild strawberries growing on the sunny side of the ridge in a little clearing in the trees.[31]

All these images, either relating to sport, holidaying or Nature, signify such forces as have their own revitalizing effect.

III

It is significant to remember that some of these images function as symbols, or at least have symbolic dimensions. 'Rain' is one of the symbols in *The Sun Also Rises,* and while usually rain stands for life, for fertility, for vegetation and growth, in the present novel it stands for minor destruction or dislocation, for gloom and bad weather:

> In the morning it was raining. A fog had come over the mountains from the sea. You could not see the tops of the mountains. The plateau was dull and gloomy, and the shapes of the trees and houses were changed. I walked out beyond the town to look at the weather. The bad weather was coming over the mountains from the sea. The flags in the square hung wet from the white poles and the banners were wet and hung dump against the front of the houses, and in between the steady drizzle the rain came down and drove everyone under the arcades and made pools of water in the square, and the streets wet and dark and deserted....[32]

It is true, as we find, that the rain causes some disturbance to the fiesta; nevertheless, the show goes on and on 'without any pause.'[33]

As we go through the present novel, we see that the game of poker dice has its own symbolical value and that the context in which it is described does impart to it a specific kind of meaningfulness:

> So we rolled poker dice out of a deep leather dice-cup. Bill was out first roll. Mike lost to me and handed the bartender a hundred-franc note. The whiskies were twelve francs apiece. We had another round and Mike lost again. Each time he gave the bartender a good tip. In a room off the bar there was a good jazz band playing. It was a pleasant bar. We had another round. I went out on the first roll with four kings. Bill and Mike rolled. Mike won the first roll with four jacks. Bill won the second. On the

> final roll Mike had three kings and let them stay. He handed the dice-cup to Bill. Bill rattled them and rolled, and there were three kings, an ace, and a queen.[34]

The fiesta at Pamplona is over; the tourists are in a mood to leave the place, and before leaving for their destinations, Jake Barnes, Mike Campbell and Bill Gorton play the game of poker dice. It is not at all difficult to see that while the three kings stand for Jake Barnes, Mike Campbell and Bill Gorton, the ace stands for Robert Cohn and the queen for Brett Ashley. Moreover, Campbell's final victory in the game of poker dice anticipates his ultimate victory in life too, for even though Robert Cohn keeps on shadowing Brett and the bull-fighter, Pedro Romero, takes her away from Mike, finally she would return to him alone.

Similarly, the picture of a khaki-clad mounted policeman directing traffic does also work as a symbol:

> Downstairs we came out through the first-floor dining-room to the street. A waiter went for a taxi. It was hot and bright. Up the street was a little square with trees and grass where there were taxis parked. A taxi came up the street, the waiter hanging out at the side. I tipped him and told the driver where to drive, and got in beside Brett. The driver started up the street. I settled back. Brett moved close to me. We set close against each other. I put my arm around her and she rested against me comfortably. It was very hot and bright, and the houses looked sharply white. We turned out on to the Gran Via.
> 'Oh, Jake,' Brett said, 'we could have had such a damned good time together.'
> Ahead was a mounted policeman in khaki directing traffic. He raised his baton. The car slowed suddenly pressing Brett against me.[35]

The policeman directs the traffic by raising his baton, but it appears to Jake Barnes and Brett Ashley who are inside a taxi that the policeman does so in a rather unconcerned manner. This unconcern on the policeman's part, in a way, symbolizes the indifferent elemental forces that, according to them, govern human activities.

It is indeed amazing that in an unobtrusive manner, Hemingway introduces two minor symbols in *The Sun Also Rises* in the form of Brett Ashley's trembling hands[36] and the scars of arrow wounds[37] on the back of Count Mippipopolous. We see, without any ambiguity whatsoever, that while Brett Ashley's trembling hands symbolize her inner weakness or brokenness, the scars of arrow wounds on the Count's back represent the widespread adverse impact that war has made on the human psyche.

'Hemingway,' says James T. Farrell, 'is a writer of limited vision, one who has no broad and fertile perspectives on life.'[38] And still *The Sun Also Rises,* is Hemingway's *Waste Land,* and Jake Barnes is his Fisher King. This may be a wild surmise or a sweeping generalization, but Philip Young says something in this connection that is indeed very useful. He says: '...once again here is the protagonist gone impotent, and his land gone sterile. Eliot's London is Hemingway's Paris, where spiritual life in general, and Jake's sexual life in particular, are alike impoverished. Prayer breaks down and falls, a knowledge of traditional distinctions between good and evil is largely lost, copulation is morally neutral and, cut off from the past chiefly by the spiritual disaster of the war, life has become mostly meaningless. "What shall we do?" is the same constant question, to which the answer must be, again, "Nothing." To hide it, instead of playing chess one drinks, mechanically and always. Love is a possibility only for the two who cannot love; once again homosexuality intensifies this atmosphere of sterility; once more the Fisher King is also a man who fishes.'[39] However, in Eliot's *Waste Land,* Philip Young goes on to say, 'A message of salvation comes out of the life-giving rain which falls on western civilization. In Hemingway's waste land there is fun, but there is no hope. No rain falls on Europe this time....'[40]

In his turn, Mark Spilka observes that Hemingway designs 'an extensive parable'[41] in *The Sun Also Rises.* In this novel,

Spilka further says, 'His protagonists are deliberately shaped as allegorical figures: Jake Barnes and Brett Ashley are two lovers desexed by the war: Robert Cohn is the false knight who challenges their despair; while Romero, the stalwart bull-fighter, personifies the good life which will survive their failure. Of course, these characters are not abstractions in the text; they are realized through the most concrete style in American fiction, and their larger meaning is implied by their response to immediate situations. But the implications are there, the parable is at work in every scene, and its presence lends unity and depth to the whole novel.'[42]

It is important to realize that the true allegorical or symbolical significance of *The Sun Also Rises* lies contained in its title. This title has been taken from *Ecclesiastes* of the *Old Testament,* and the relevant lines are as follows:

> The word of the Preacher, the son of David, king in Jerusalem.
>
> Vanity of vanities, saith the Preacher, vanity of vanities; all is vanity. What profit hath a man of all his labour which he taketh under the sun?
>
> One generation passeth away, and another generation cometh; but the earth abideth for ever.
>
> The sun also ariseth, and the sun also goeth down, and hasteth to his place where he arose.[43]

All things belonging to this world are mere vanity, in fact, vautiy of vanities. People go on toiling all through their lives, but they hardly get anything out of what they do. No doubt, people come and go; the sun appears and disappears; the wind blows to and fro; everything is perishable, and yet, says the Preacher, the earth abides for ever. There is a good deal of frustration and perversion and disenchantment in *The Sun Also Rises;* the whole climate, the very atmosphere of this novel is dominated by excessive drinking, meaningless holidaying and promiscuity, and yet the picture of the Irati riverside and that of the carefree and dancing Basque people make us believe that all is not yet over, that there is still some room for hope, and that in spite of all infection and sickness and morbidity, the earth will abide for ever. In this context we have to take special note of the way Hemingway describes the gaiety of the Basque peasants, raw and vigorous and virile:

> People were coming into the square from all sides, and down the street we heard the pipes and the fifes and the drums coming. They were playing the *riau-riau* music, the pipes shrill and the drums pounding, and behind them came the men and boys dancing. When the fifers stopped they all crouched down in the street, and when the reed-pipes and the fifes shrilled, and the flat, dry hollow drums tapped it out again, they all went up in the air dancing. In the crowd you saw only the heads and shoulders of the dancers going up and down.[44]

The psychological, the spiritual darkness is there; Hemingway makes use of the word 'dark'[45] several times in the novel in both its physical and spiritual sense, and still he describes the 'sun'[46] as an object, a symbol of light and life, as a force or phenomenon that makes everything 'bright'[47] and 'radiant.'[48]

IV

Considered as a novel, *The Sun Also Rises* may seem to be 'a slight thing;'[49] at times it may even be dismissed as 'an immoral book'[50] chiefly for the reason that the world of this novel is a world of drunken promiscuity, and yet we cannot and should not lose sight of the fact that Hemingway did have his own interest in the problem of the meaning and values of human life, that his is 'an intensely implicational'[51] mode of writing in spite of his austere and sparse style, that he 'rarely interprets his juxtapositions for us,'[52] that his novels do contain 'submerged'[53] meanings, and that his images to function as the 'symbols of an inner world.'[54] Mark Spilka says the very same thing in a different way when he states that 'with Hemingway, the great outdoors is chiefly a state of mind, a projection of moral and emotional attitudes on to physical arenas, so that a clear account of surface action will reproduce these attitudes in the reader.'[55]

As we have said earlier, it is for quite understandable reasons that we find images of emptiness in *The Sun Also Rises,* but it is also equally understandable that these images of emptiness are generally followed by those of cleansing, mopping up or sweeping. Similarly, quite a few of the other images that we get in the present novel relate chiefly to the false knight, Robert Cohn, though there are some that take us straight on to the bull-fighter, Pedro Romero. In the preceding pages, we have also discussed at some length the importance of such images as present to us an integrated picture of happiness, growth and fruitfulness amidst despair, decay and degeneration. It is in this very light that we have to interpret the goat image and the images pertaining to bull-fight and fishing.

At this point it is important to refer to the suggestiveness of some of the symbols—the symbol of rain, the symbol of the game of poker dice, the symbol of a mounted policeman directing traffic, the symbol of Brett Ashley's trembling hands and the symbol of the scars of arrow wounds on the Count's back in particular—that we get in *The Sun Also Rises.* We have also considered the present novel as a parable, as an extended parable in fact, in which images and symbols do have their own value, and we have as well tried to bring out the allegorical significance of the title of this novel, which has been taken from *Ecclesiastes* of the *Old Testament* and which suggests that though all is vanity, vanity of vanities really, the earth abides for ever.

It is sometimes contended that since Hemingway was concerned chiefly with the representation of 'the real thing'[56] and wanted to state the whole thing in a direct and straightforward manner, there is hardly any room for the intentional use of symbols in his novels. And though to a certain extent, this attitude may be correct, yet we do come across images and symbols in his writings. However, there are two things that have to be taken note of in this connection. The first is that Hemingway makes use of his symbols so skilfully and so unobtrusively that they do not seem to have been used at all.

And, secondly, most of the symbols in his novels are used in the form of images; his images do have their own symbolic value, and it is indeed very difficult to draw a line of distinction between his images and his symbols.

REFERENCES

1. James T. Farrell, *The League of Frightened Philistines* (New York, 1945), 20.
2. Philip Young, *Ernest Hemingway* (New York, 1952), 59.
3. Ernest Hemingway, *The Sun Also Rises* (Penguin edition 1974), 17.
4. James T. Farrell, *The League of Frightened Philistines* (New York, 1945), 21.
5. Charles Shapiro (ed.), *Twelve Original Essays on Great American Novels* (Detroit, 1958), 245.
6. Ernest Hemingway, *The Sun Also Rises* (Penguin edition, 1974), 36.
7. Hemingway 36.
8. Hemingway 115.
9. Hemingway 174.
10. Hemingway 177.
11. Hemingway 144.
12. Hemingway 9.
13. Hemingway 9.
14. Hemingway 11.
15. Hemingway 148.
16. Hemingway 149.
17. Hemingway 148.
18. Hemingway 22.
19. Hemingway 12.
20. Hemingway 146.
21. C. Shapiro (ed.), *Twelve Original Essays on Great American Novels* (Detroit, 1958), 251.
22. Ernest Hemingway, *The Sun Also Rises* (Penguin edition, 1974), 39.
23. Hemingway 38.
24. C. Shapiro (ed.), *Twelve Original Essays on Great American Novels* (Detroit, 1958), 241.
25. Hemingway, *The Sun Also Rises* (Penguin edition, 1974), 133.
26. Hemingway 142.

27. Hemingway 142.
28. Hemingway 97.
29. Hemingway 118-9.
30. Hemingway 87.
31. Hemingway 90-91.
32. Hemingway 130.
33. Hemingway 130.
34. Hemingway 175.
35. Hemingway 189.
36. Hemingway 141.
37. Hemingway 50.
38. James T. Farrell, *The League of Frightened Philistines* (New York, 1945), 22.
39. P. Young, *Ernest Hemingway* (New York, 1952), 59-60.
40. Young 60.
41. C. Shapiro (ed.), *Twelve Original Essays on Great American Novels* (Detroit, 1958), 239.
42. Shapiro 239.
43. *The Holy Bible* (Cambridge, n.d.), 699.
44. Ernest Hemingway, *The Sun Also Rises* (Penguin edition, 1974), 118.
45. Hemingway 119.
46. Hemingway 159.
47. Hemingway 159.
48. Hemingway 159.
49. E. Wagenknecht, *Cavalcade of the American Novel* (Calcutta, 1952), 369.
50. Wagenknecht 375.
51. Wagenknecht 372.
52. Wagenknecht 372.
53. See George Hemphill, 'Hemingway and James,' *Kenyon Review,* XI (1949), 50-60.
54. See Introduction to Malcolm Cowley, *Ernest Hemingway: The Man and His Work* (New York, 1944), 316-17.
55. C. Shapiro (ed.), *Twelve Original Essays on Great American Novels* (Detroit, 1958), 245.
56. Ernest Hemingway, *Death in the Afternoon* (Penguin edition, 1966), 6.

3

A Farewell to Arms

A FAREWELL to Arms came out in 1929, and it proved to be an instant success. Hemingway's first three books, *In Our Time*, *The Sun Also Rises* and the present novel deal substantially with the same problem: the predicament of man in a society rocked by the violence of war. However, leaving aside *In Our Time*, a collection of precariously connected short stories, we do notice a vital point of difference between *The Sun Also Rises* and *A Farewell to Arms*. In his article on *A Farewell to Arms,* Ray B. West Jr. puts the whole thing so very clearly and significantly when he says: '*The Sun Also Rises*, although set in the postwar period, is conditioned by the wartime disability of its principal figure, Jake Barnes. But the setting for *A Farewell to Arms* is the war itself, and the romance of Frederic Henry and Catherine Barkley, their attempt to escape the war and its resulting chaos, is a parable of twentieth-century man's disgust and disillusionment at the failure of civilization to achieve the ideals it had been promising throughout the nineteenth century.'[1] Moreover, *A Farewell to Arms* is a very well-written novel, a novel that does have its own order and sequence, a novel containing five separate books, each book composed of a series of scenes, and each scene broken meaningfully into sections. In Book I we are introduced to all important characters of this novel, besides being acquainted with the concerned problem or problems; Book II records the development in the romance between Frederic Henry and Catherine Barkley; in Book III we see the retreat taking place at Caporetto and take note of Henry's decision to escape the disorder and confusion of war; Book IV takes us to Switzerland where Frederic Henry and Catherine Barkley find themselves in a state of supposed safety, while in Book V everything ends up tragically with the death of Catherine Barkley during childbirth. *A Farewell to Arms* has the intensity of a tragic play; quite characteristically, it brings us face-to-face with a queer reversal of situation, and it does contain a lot of images and symbols that have to be examined, analysed and explained with care and attention.

It is the title of the novel, *A Farewell to Arms*, itself that first catches our attention. The obvious and ready implication of the title may be that since Frederic has deserted the army and, in a way, successfully escaped from the disorder and barbarism of war, he has given a farewell to arms, to war. But in that event we have to accept the present novel as just a war novel, and we know that *A Farewell to Arms* is not merely a war novel. Then again, the title of this novel may also imply a farewell to the arms of Catherine, and in this case, the title would point to Catherine's death and, thus, to the tragic loss of Frederic's love. However, these two interpretations of the title amount to our taking a very constricted view of the novel. The truth is that the title of *A Farewell to Arms* is a masterstroke of irony and that we have to think seriously in terms of offering an ironic interpretation of the title.

Frederic, it seems, has always tried to run away from the obligations and responsibilities of life. He did not want to fall in love, and yet he fell in love with Catherine. He escaped from war and Catherine gave up her job at the hospital in the hope that they would be able to lead a peaceful life, a life devoid of conflict and tension and struggle. However, Catherine's death during labour is a firm pointer to the suggestion that it is difficult, if not impossible, for man to have a separate peace with life, a kind of peace that is supposed to result from escape, and that man has to learn to live with life and endure it. It is in this sense that we have to appreciate the suggestiveness of the title of *A Farewell to Arms*.

II

It is something really important and interesting to see that in *A Farewell to Arms* Hemingway makes a very intricate but meaningful combination of images and symbols in order to be able to express whatever he has to convey to his readers. There is no mistaking the point that there is a close connection between man and nature in the present novel and that it is in this regard that we identify 'rain' as the first among the important symbols in this novel. In fact, rain is a recurring symbol in the novel, and the word 'rain' itself occurs at so many places in the book. However, wherever and whenever we come across 'rain' in *A Farewell to Arms*, it invariably stands for disease and sickness, want and scarcity, misery and misfortune, gloom and depression, fear and insecurity, darkness and destruction. In the very opening pages of the novel, Hemingway speaks about 'the permanent rain' that causes cholera and spells disaster:

> At the start of the winter came the permanent rain and with the rain came the cholera. But it was checked and in the end only seven thousand died of it in the army.[2]

It is something really significant to note that in the following piece of conversation between Frederic and Catherine, 'rain' is associated with the latter's sense of fear:

> 'You're not really afraid of the rain, are you?'
>
> 'Not when I'm with you.'
>
> 'Why are you afraid of it?'
>
> 'I don't know.'
>
> 'Tell me.'
>
> 'Don't make me.'
>
> 'Tell me.'
>
> 'No.'
>
> 'Tell me.'
>
> 'All right. I'm afraid of the rain because sometimes I see me dead in it.'
>
> 'No.'
>
> 'And sometimes I see you dead in it.'[3]

And in spite of all assurances and comforts that Frederic gives her, Catherine keeps on crying because of the fear of 'rain':

> It's all nonsense. It's only nonsense. I'm not afraid of the rain, Oh, oh, God, I wish I wasn't. She was crying.[4]

'Rain', we find, does also stand for separation, for it is in the rain that Frederic leaves Catherine behind at Milan on his way to the battle front:

> 'Good-bye,' I said. I stepped out into the rain and the carriage started. Catherine learned out and I saw her face in the light. She smiled and waved. The carriage went up the street, Catherine pointed in toward the archway. I looked, there were only the two carabiniere and the archway, I realized she meant for me to get in out of the rain. I went in and stood and watched the carriage turn the corner. Then I started through the station and down the runway to the train.[5]

It is important to see that the retreat of the Italian army, taking place at Gorizia, is accompanied by rain:

> The next night the retreat started. We heard that Germans and Austrians had broken through in the north and were coming down the mountain valleys toward Cividale and Udine. The retreat was orderly, wet and sullen. In the night, going slowly along the crowded roads we passed troops marching under the rain, guns, horses pulling wagons, mules, motor trucks all moving away from the front. There was no more disorder than in an advance.[6]

Similarly, as Frederic and Catherine try to escape to Switzerland across the lake in a boat, their journey is lashed by rains, and they stand in danger of losing sense of direction:

> 'What time is it?' Catherine asked.
>
> 'It's only eleven o' clock,' I said.
>
> 'If you row all the time you ought to be there by seven o'clock in the morning.'
>
> 'Is it that far?'
>
> 'It's thirty-five kilometres.'
>
> 'How should we go? In this rain we need a compass.'[7]

And it is in the rain that Frederic walks back to his hotel, leaving Catherine behind at the hospital, dead and lifeless:

> ...after I had got them out and shut the door and turned off the light it wasn't any good. It was like saying good-bye to a statue. After a while I went out and left the hospital and walked back to the hospital in the rain.[8]

It is not at all difficult to see that in *A Farewell to Arms,* 'rain' does also stand for death and destruction.

The whole implication of 'rain' as a symbol becomes much clearer in view of the fact that as Frederic and Catherine reach the Switzerland coast, the author comments: 'there was a fine November rain falling but it looked cheerful and clean even with the rain.'[9] In his book, *Hemingway: The Writer as Artist*, Carlos Baker says that in *A Farewell to Arms,* 'natural elements take on a symbolic function,'[10] that the short first chapter of this novel 'closes with winter, and the establishment of rain as a symbol of disaster,'[11] and that the 'use of rain as a kind of symbolic obligato in the novel had been widely and properly admired.'[12]

In fact, as Baker puts it, 'There is hardly a natural beauty in the whole first chapter of *A Farewell to Arms* which has not some symbolic function in Hemingway's first study in doom.'[13] In the late summer, there is dust that, being stirred by the breeze, powders the leaves of the trees: in the autumn the leaves dry out, fall, decay, and become part of the dust, and as the troops march through this bare and austere landscape, the words of the funeral service do necessarily remind as that, like the fallen and falling leaves, the marching troops too are going to mingle with the dust, some of them soon, most of them eventually.

Like the rain and the dust and the fallen and falling leaves, the river too is a major symbol in *A Farewell to Arms*. In the course of their retreat, the Italian troops are to move back beyond the river Tagliamento at Caporetto. Frederic too joins the retreat with the other members of his ambulance unit; but as he comes to the bridge over Tagliamento and watches the security guards stationed there checking and interrogating the retreating troops, he fears that, being an American and not an Italian, he may be looked upon as a suspect and placed under arrest or killed. Frederic is much too desperate to brook any delay; he is so keen on getting back his freedom, meeting Catherine, and spending the rest of his life with her in safety, and it is in this mood that, even though the river is in spate, he jumps into it: 'I ducted down, pushed between two men, and ran for the river, my head down. I tripped at the edge and went in with a splash. The water was very cold and I stayed under as long as I could.'[14] Frederic's plunge into the river is a leap into freedom and safety. The symbol of timber, a conventional symbol indeed, that we find in the following passage, lends solidity and substance to the symbol of river as an agent of freedom and security:

> When I came up the second time I saw a piece of timber ahead of me and reached it and held on with one hand. I kept my head behind it and did not even look over it. I did not want to see the bank.... The piece of timber swung in the current and I held it with one hand. I looked at the bank. It seemed to be going by very fast.... I held on to the timber with both hands and let it take me along. The shore was out of sight now.[15]

Moreover, Frederic's plunge into the river is a kind of baptism, an initiation into a new kind of life, a life far removed from dirt and filth and blood and violence. Frederic's 'anger,' says Hemingway, 'was washed away in the river along with any obligation.'[16] In this connection Ray B. West Jr. observes:

> Malcolm Cowley has likened Fredric's plunge into the river to escape execution as a baptism—a symbol of Frederic's entering the world of the initiated, but this is true only in so far as it refers to his decision (his rebirth) concerning the war. The chapters preceding, where Frederic returns to the front and meets his old comrades, indicate both how much he had learned through his stay at the hospital (the baptism of love) and how much the members of his company have learned through the difficult fighting of the summer (their baptism of fire), but the final consecration does not come until later when

> Frederic is confronted by love and death at the same time.[17]

And he goes on to say: 'The retreat does, however, represent a major phase in his initiation.'[18]

It is important to remember that we have to consider most of the images and symbols in Hemingway's novels in general and in *A Farewell to Arms* in particular in the context of special situations therein, and it is perhaps thus that we may best bring out their significance and value. Frederic has left war at a great risk to himself to enter the world of love, but now that Catherine is about to die at the hospital, with the newly-delivered baby already dead, everything appears to be so grim and dark and futile to him. At this hour, he is completely overwhelmed by a feeling of helplessness, and it is in this light that we have to examine this symbol of log, full of ants, on top of the fire. The whole scene, we find, comes to Frederic as a piece of remembrance:

> Once in camp I put a log on top of the fire and it was full of ants. As it commenced to burn, the ants swarmed out and went first towards the centre where the fire was, then turned back and ran towards the end. When there were enough on the end they fell off into the fire. Some got out, their bodies burnt and flattened, and went off not knowing where they were going. But most of them went toward the fire and then back toward the end and swarmed on the cool end and finally fell off into the fire. I remember thinking at the time that it was the end of the world and a splendid chance to be a messiah and lift the log off the fire and throw it out where the ants could get off into the ground. But I did not do anything but throw a tin cup of water on the log, so that I would have the cup empty to put whisky in before I added water to it. I think the cup of water on the burning log only steamed the ants.[19]

The relationship of this parable to Catherine's predicament, we see, is unmistakable, for just as Frederic does not play the role of a messiah in respect of the ants, similarly there is no messiah to come to Catherine's rescue. Death is the end of every human life, and the only value attached to death is man's knowledge of it. Frederic learns about war, about love, and finally about death, and Catherine's death is the final stage in his initiation.

It is only proper that in his comments on *A Farewell to Arms,* Charles R. Anderson speaks of 'the novel's weather symbolism'[20] as well as of the 'muted lyricism'[21] of Hemingway's prose in it, that Carlos Baker tells us about the presence of 'elemental images'[22] in *A Farewell to Arms*, and that E.M. Halliday tries to make us aware of Hemingway's 'manner of implication,'[23] of his use of 'the symbolism of association to convey by implication'[24] the essential meaning of his novels and short stories. In *A Farewell to Arms*, as we see, war itself, standing for disorder and violence and destruction, is 'a symbol for the chaos of nature'[25] in which Frederic is trapped. It is really characteristic of Hemingway that he adopts the controlling technique of understatement in his use of symbolism, and typically enough, Frederic feels embarrassed at the use of big words:

> I was always embarrassed by the words sacred, glorious, and sacrifice and the expression in vain. We had heard them, sometimes standing in the rain almost out of earshot, so that only the shouted words came through, and had read them, on proclamations that were slapped up by billposters over other proclamations.... Abstract words such as glory, honour, courage, or hallow were obscene beside the concrete names of villages, the numbers of roads, the names of rivers, the numbers of regiments and the dates.[26]

It is in this spirit that we have to view a particular lake, Lake Maggiore as a symbol:

> He bent down and shoved us off. I dug at the water with the oars, then waved one hand. The barman waved back deprecatingly. I saw the lights of the hotel and rowed out, rowing straight out until they were out of sight. There was quite a sea running but we were going with the wind.[27]

This lake, spreading out between Stresa and Switzerland, may be viewed as an instrument of safety, for it is by rowing through this very lake that Frederic and Catherine are able to reach the shore of safety in Switzerland.

There is a very meaningful doctor-priest contrast in *A Farewell to Arms* that does have its own bearing on at least one important aspect of this novel. Frederic is to go on leave, and several of his friends and colleagues advise him to go to different places. However, the priest wants him to go to Abruzzi, which is his own place, while the captain, Dr. Rinaldi, is so very impatient about his visit to the whore-house:

> 'I would like you to go to Abruzzi,' the priest said. The others were shouting. 'There is good hunting. You would like the people and though it is cold it is clear and dry. You could stay with my family. My father is a famous hunter.'
>
> 'Come on,' said the captain.
>
> 'We go whore-house before it shuts.'
>
> 'Good night,' I said to the priest.
>
> 'Good night,' he said.[28]

And because Frederic is not able to go to Abruzzi where 'though it is cold, it is clear and dry,' he feels terribly sad and sorry about his failure to do so. He thinks:

> I had wanted to go to Abruzzi. I had gone to no place where the roads were frozen and hard as iron, where it was clear cold and dry and the snow was dry and powdery and hare-tracks in the snow and the peasants took off their hats and called you Lord and there was good hunting. I had gone to no such place but to the smoke of cafés and nights when the room whirled and you needed to look at the wall to make it stop, nights in bed, drunk, when you knew that that was all there was, and the strange excitement of waking and not knowing who it was with you, and the world all unreal in the dark and so exciting that you must resume again unknowing and not caring in the night, sure that this was all and all and all and not caring.[29]

The priest's religion is his cold but clear and dry country; the doctor has his own interest in the whorehouse, while Frederic has his cafés and exciting nights. *A Farewell to Arms* is not a religious novel; nevertheless, it is a novel of religious consciousness. The priest is already there in the novel, and Catherine Barkley speaks to Frederic Henry in the language of religion when she tells him: 'You're my religion. You're all l've got.'[30] It is indeed true that Frederic has nothing to do with religion as such: at best, his religious sensibility is utterly limited, and yet when Catherine is dying at the hospital during childbirth, he weeps and prays to God in the most desperate of terms:

> Don't let her die. Oh, God, please don't let her die. I'II do anything for you if you won't let her die. Please, please, please, dear God, don't let her die. Dear God, don't let her die. Please, please, please, don't let her die. God, please make her not die. I'll do anything you say if you don't let her die.... Please, dear God, don't let her die.[31]

It is not without significance that Frederic turns to God at this moment of terrible grief.

Frederic's religious sensibility which is a symbol for the religious sensibility of our time, is further brought into focus by the incident that takes place near the church:

> There were street-car tracks and beyond them was the cathedral....
>
> 'Would you like to go in!'
>
> 'No,' Catherine said. We walked along. There was a soldier standing with his girl in the shadow of one of the stone buttresses ahead of us and we passed them. They were standing tight up against the stone and he had put his cape around her.
>
> 'They're like us,' I said.
>
> 'Nobody is like us,' Catherine said. She did not mean it happily.
>
> 'I wish they had some place to go.'
>
> 'It mightn't do them any good.'

> 'I don't know. Everybody ought to have some place to go.'
>
> 'They have the cathedral,' Catherine said.[32]

As Frederic Henry is about to leave for the battle front, he and Catherine pass beside a cathedral during rain. However, while they see a soldier and his girl taking shelter in the cathedral, they themselves do not take shelter there; instead, they go to their hotel room in Milan. Typically enough, Fredric is a hero who finds himself swinging to and fro between two worlds, the world of tradition and the world of uncertainty. And it is perhaps in terms of religious consciousness that we find both Dr. Rinaldi and Catherine's nurse-friend, Fergusson, making use of snake as a symbol. Quite interestingly, Rinaldi calls himself 'the snake,'[33] 'the snake of reason,'[34] in fact, while Fergusson looks upon Frederic as snake for having seduced Catherine. She tells Frederic: 'You're worse than sneaky. You're like a snake. A snake with an Italian uniform: with a cape around your neck.'[35]

In his book entitled *Hemingway: The Writer as Artist,* Carlos Baker maintains that in *A Farewell to Arms* 'the plain and the mountains (not to mention the river and the trees, the dust and the leaves) have a fundamental value as symbols'[36] and that throughout the substructure of the book, these two symbols are opposed to each other. He observes:

> Despite the insistent denotative matter-of-factness at the surface of the presentation, the subsurface activity of *A Farewell to Arms* is organized connotatively around two poles. By a process of accrual and coagulation, the images tend to build round the opposed concepts of Home and Not-Home. Neither, of course, is truly conceptualistic; each is a kind of poetic intuition, charged with emotional values and woven; like a cable, of many strands. The Home-concept, for example, is associated with the mountains; with dry-cold weather; with peace and quiet; with love, dignity, health, happiness, and the good life; and with worship or at least the consciousness of God. The Not-Home concept is associated with low-lying plains: with rain and fog; with obscenity, indignity,

> disease, suffering, nervousness, war and death; and with irreligion.[37]

Baker stresses this very point further when he states: 'The total structure of the novel is developed, in fact, around the series of contrasting situations.... To Gorizia, the Not-Home of war, succeeds the Home which Catherine and Frederic make together in the Milan Hospital. The Not-Home of the grim retreat from Isonzo is followed by the quiet and happy retreat which the loves share above Montreux. Home ends for Frederic Henry when he leaves Catherine dead in the Lausanne Hospital.'[38] And finally, referring to 'that special combination of naturalistic and symbolic truth-telling'[39] which is so very peculiar to Hemingway's art, Baker states:

> Projected in actualistic terms and a matter-of-fact tone, telling the truth about the effects of war in human life, *A Farewell to Arms* is entirely and even exclusively acceptable as a naturalistic narrative of what happened. To read it only as such, however, is to miss its controlling symbolism: the deep central antithesis between the image of life and home (the mountain) and the image of war and death (the plain).[40]

Baker, we see, repeatedly lays stress on the Home and Not-Home symbols.

In his essay captioned 'Hemingway's Ambiguity: Symbolism and Irony,' E.M. Halliday examines Carols Baker's interpretation of the symbolism in *A Farewell to Arms*. He says: 'Professor Carlos Baker...has established himself as the leading oracle of Hemingway's symbolism. His book, *Hemingway: The Writer as Artist*, is, I think, the most valuable piece of extended Hemingway criticism that we yet have, and to a large extent its contribution is one of new insights into the symbolist aspect of his subject's narrative method.'[41] He admits that Baker's 'chapter on *A Farewell to Arms* is an original piece of criticism'[42] and that the deep central antithesis between the mountains and the plain as symbols 'cannot be denied...by anyone with an acceptable understanding of the book.'[43] However, according to Halliday, the 'question at issue is one of technique: to what extent, and how precisely, is the central antithesis in fact engineered around the Mountain and the Plain as symbols?'[44] Halliday argues over again and again to drive the point home to us that in *A Farewell to Arms,* the mountains do not always symbolize Home and that the plain does not always stand for Not-Home. It is thus that he calls Baker's interpretation of symbolism in *A Farewell to Arms* a 'greatly overelaborated critical gimmick,'[45] and states that nowhere in the novel does Hemingway 'set up the artificially rigid and unrealistic contrast between the Mountain and the Plain which Mr. Baker's analysis requires.'[46] Halliday maintains that the essential feature of Hemingway's art is not so much symbolism as what he calls 'the ambiguity of reason.'[47]

Halliday tries to take a balanced view of Hemingway's narrative art when he observes:

> It would be foolish to argue that the work of any first-rate writer owes its success exclusively or even predominantly to any one narrative artifice. Hemingway has used techniques of symbolism and techniques of irony and used them well: what we want in criticism is an even view of his use of these and other artistic resources that does not exaggerate one at the expense of others.[48]

It is clear that even though Halliday attaches greater importance to irony than to symbolism in respect of Hemingway's narrative art, with certain reservations he does accept the validity of the mountains and the plain as the two major symbols in *A Farewell to Arms*.

III

Besides these symbols in *A Farewell to Arms*, we do also find in this novel a number of other images that, in their own ways, contribute substantially to its symbolical or metaphorical make-up. Frederic has been making advances to Catherine Barkley when both are off their duty; it is Dr. Rinaldi, a habitual visitor to the whorehouse, who has introduced Frederic to her, and in his turn Frederic loses no time in courting her, perhaps taking her lightly and not exactly knowing what he is really up to:

> I leaned forward in the dark to kiss her and there was a sharp stinging flash. She had slapped my face hard. Her hand had hit my nose and eyes, and tears came in my eyes from the reflex. 'I' m so sorry,' she said. I felt I had a certain advantage.
> 'You were quite right.'
> 'I'm dreadfully sorry,' she said. 'I just couldn't stand the nurse's-evening-off aspect of it. I didn't mean to hurt you. I did hurt you, didn't I?'
> She was looking at me in the dark. I was angry and yet certain, seeing it all ahead like the moves in a chess game.[49]

It is both natural and proper that because of his lustful and unthinking behaviour with Catherine, Frederic is compared to 'a dog in heat':

> After a while I walked with her to the door of the villa and she went in and I walked home. Back at the villa I went upstairs to the room. Rinaldi was lying on his bed. He looked at me.
> 'So you make progress with Miss Barkley?'
> 'We are friends.'
> 'You have that pleasant air of a dog in heat.'[50]

For the present, Frederic does not think in terms of love or companionship for life: he is interested, more or less, in sheer physical sensations, though he does like Catherine, and it is for his silly gamesomeness that Hemingway employs the image of the game of bridge:

> I knew I did not love Catherine Barkley nor had any idea of loving her. This was a game, like bridge, in which you said things instead of playing cards. Like bridge, you had to pretend you were playing for money or playing for some stakes. Nobody had mentioned what the stakes were. It was all right with me.[51]

It is indeed a pity that though Frederic has been playing without any stakes in respect of Catherine Barkley, he does not know, in fact he cannot know, at this moment that the stakes are going to be really very high. These three images are all of a piece, bound inextricably together by the nature of Frederic's initial encounter with Catherine.

However, as the relations between Frederic Henry and Catherine Barkley develop and grow deeper, they find it difficult to bear the pang of separation. Catherine has been working at a hospital away from Frederic who is engaged in his duties at the battle front. And when they meet after a certain period of separation, it is quite understandable that Hemingway employs another set of images to bring out their feeling of happiness at their reunion. 'It was as though,' think both Frederic and Catherine, 'we met again after each of us had been away on a long journey.'[52] As Catherine goes upstairs to see Frederic there at the Milan hospital, it appears to him as if she 'had been away on a long trip.'[53] And when they are together in a room, even though at the hospital, they get a queer feeling of being 'inside a tent or behind a falls.'[54]

However, it is the feeling of distress and despair and loneliness and insecurity that pervades the narrative of *A Farewell to Arms.* The row of beautiful but cold marble busts at the hospital reminds Frederic of 'cemetry,'[55] and the image of the worn-out carpet[56] at the hotel in Milan where Frederic and Catherine are staying represents the process of decay that is associated with war. The image of a dog searching for something in the empty cans points to the futility of human pursuit:

> Outside along the street were the refuse cans from the houses waiting for the collector. A dog was nosing at one of the cans.
>
> 'What do you want?' I asked and looked in the can to see if there was anything I could pull out for him; there was nothing on top but coffee-grounds, dust and some dead flowers.
>
> 'There isn't anything, dog,' I said.[57]

At this moment, Frederic is haunted by a feeling of nothingness. And, similarly, the image of a pile of empty saucers on the table in front of Frederic is a reminder of the emptiness of life, for this image of empty saucers and glasses, as we have discussed earlier, occurs several times in *The Sun Also Rises* too.[58]

Most of these images are used in *A Farewell to Arms* at a time when Frederic and Catherine's child, looking like 'a freshly-skinned rabbit.'[59] has been born dead, and when Catherine herself has been struggling for her life at the hospital. The team of doctors and nurses, wearing marks, appears to Frederic to be something like 'a drawing of the Inquisition,'[60] and at the same time the stitching of Catherine's wound does also remind Frederic of a cobbler's stitching:

> I thought Catherine was dead. She looked dead. Her face was grey, the part of it that I could see. Down below, under the light, the doctor was sewing up the great long, force-spread, thick-edged wound. Another doctor in a mask gave the anaesthetic. Two nurses in masks handed things. It looked like a drawing of the Inquisition. I knew as I watched I could have watched it all, but I was glad I hadn't. I do not think I could have watched them cut, but I watched the wound closed into a high welted ridge with quick skilful-looking stitches like a cobblers....[61]

It is Frederic's reaction to the supposed rawness and cruelty of the scene that explains the use of these images. They evoke a particular state of mind in a particular situation.

It is in this very light that we have to consider the image of a statue for which, in a way, Hemingway prepares us by way of the image of cemetry mentioned earlier:

> ...after I had got them out and shut the door and turned off the light it wasn't any good. It was like saying good-bye to a statue. After a while I went out and left the hospital and walked back to the hotel in the rain.[62]

Catherine Barkley is dead. Frederic Henry has lost her and the baby too. He has shut himself up for sometime in the room where Catherine is lying dead. Light and darkness do not make any difference to her now, and everything, every kind of persuasion, of entreaty, of coaxing is now immaterial to her. Frederic is left with no choice but to leave her there and walk out of the room. 'The loved woman,' says Baker, 'has become in death an abstract unvital image of her living self, a marble memorial to all that has gone without hope of recovery.'[63] And he goes on to say: 'Her death completes the symbolic structure, the edifice of tragedy so carefully erected. This structure is essentially poetic in conception and execution.'[64]

A Farewell to Arms may be explained, as is usually done, in realistic terms, for, besides other things, it does deal with the effect of war on human life, with what happened to a small group of people on the Italian front during 1917-18. This novel may also be interpreted as a work of fiction that seeks to draw our attention, as James F. Light says, to 'the four ideals of service.'[65] He observes:

> Each of these ideals is dramatized by a character of some importance, and it is between these four that Lt. Henry wavers in the course of the novel. The orthodoxy religious ideal of service is that of the Priest.... Another selfless ideal of service is that of the patriot Gino.... A third is the code of Catherine Barkley who wishes to serve her lover and who sees in such service her personal substitute for conventional religion. The last is the ideal of Rinaldi who, as a doctor, wishes to serve mankind by alleviating the wounds of war.[66]

However, this idealistic stance of the book may not preclude our looking at it in terms of its ironic suggestiveness. E.M. Halliday observes: 'The ironic gap between expectation and fulfilment, pretense and fact, intention and action, the message sent and the message received, the way thing are thought or ought to be and the way things are—this has been Hemingway's great theme from the beginning; and it has called for an ironic method to do it artistic justice.'[67]

Nevertheless, its realism, its supposed commitment to idealism, or its ironic mode of presentation 'ought not finally to obscure the symbolic mythos on which it [*A Farewell to Arms*] is built and from which a great part of its emotional power derives.'[68]

Some of the more important symbols—the symbol of rain, of the dust, of the fallen and falling leaves, of the river, of the log of wood, full of ants, on top of the fire—that we have explained in the preceding pages form part of the weather or nature symbolism which is indeed so very vital for the texture of this novel. And some of the major images—the image of the game of chess and of bride, the image of a dog in heat, the image of arrival after a long trip, the image of cemetery and of the worn carpet, the image of empty cans and saucers, the image of a drawing of the Inquisition and the image of a statue—do substantially contribute to the symbolical make-up of *A Farewell to Arms*.

At this point, as we have discussed earlier, we cannot do without referring to 'the central antithesis between the image of life, love, and home (the mountain) and the image of war and death (the plain)'[69] which Carlos Baker explains in so great a detail and in which, according to him, Catherine 'has a symbolic part to play.'[70]

A Farewell to Arms is indeed a highly symbolical novel, and we have to consider it as such. In fact, it is a dexterous combination of realism and symbolism that accounts for the success of this novel as a work of art.

REFERENCES

1. R.B. West Jr. & R.W. Stallman (eds.), *The Art of Modern Fiction* (New York, 1949), 622.
2. Ernest Hemingway, *A Farewell to Arms* (Penguin edition, 1975), 8.
3. Hemingway 100.
4. Hemingway 100.
5. Hemingway 124-25.
6. Hemingway 146.
7. Hemingway 247.
8. Hemingway 256.
9. Hemingway 214.
10. C. Baker, *Hemingway; The Writer as Artist* (Princeton, 1956), 95.
11. Baker 95.

12. Baker 105.
13. Baker 95-96.
14. Ernest Hemingway, *A Farewell to Arms* (Penguin edition, 1975), 176.
15. Hemingway 176.
16. Hemingway 181.
17. R.B. West Jr. & R.W. Stallman (eds.), *The Art of Modern Fiction* (New York, 1949), 628.
18. West Jr. & R.W. Stallman 628.
19. Ernest Hemingway, *A Farewell to Arms* (Penguin edition, 1975), 252.
20. C.R. Anderson, 'Hemingway's Other Style,' *Modern Language Notes*, LXXVI (May, 1961), 439.
21. Anderson 441.
22. C. Baker, *Hemingway: The Writer as Artist* (Princeton, 1956), 94.
23. E.M. Halliday, 'Hemingway's Ambiguity: Symbolism and Irony,' *American Literature*, XXVIII (March, 1956), 4.
24. Halliday 6.
25. R.B. West Jr. & R.W. Stallman (eds.), *The Art of Modern Fiction* (New York, 1949), 630.
26. Ernest Hemingway, *A Farewell to Arms* (Penguin edition, 1975), 143-44.
27. Hemingway 208.
28. Hemingway 11.
29. Hemingway 14.
30. Hemingway 91.
31. Hemingway 254.
32. Hemingway 116.
33. Hemingway 133.
34. Hemingway 133.
35. Hemingway 190
36. C. Baker, *Hemingway: The Writer as Artist* (Princeton, 1956), 94.
37. Baker 101.
38. Baker 104.
39. Baker 115.
40. Baker 108-109.
41. E.M. Halliday, 'Hemingway's Ambiguity: Symbolism and Irony,' *American Literature*, XXVIII (March, 1956), 7.
42. Halliday 8.

43. Halliday 8.
44. Halliday 8-9.
45. Halliday 13.
46. Halliday 14.
47. Halliday 21.
48. Halliday 21.
49. Ernest Hemingway, *A Farewell to Arms* (Penguin edition, 1975), 24.
50. Hemingway 25.
51. Hemingway 28.
52. Hemingway 88.
53. Hemingway 89.
54. Hemingway 89.
55. Hemingway 26.
56. Hemingway 120 and 123.
57. Hemingway 242.
58. Hemingway 253.
59. Hemingway 249.
60. Hemingway 250.
61. Hemingway 250.
62. Hemingway 256
63. C. Baker, *Hemingway: The Writer as Artist* (Princeton, 1956), 116.
64. Ernest Hemingway, *A Farewell to Arms* (Penguin edition, 1975), 116.
65. J.F. Light, 'The Religion of Death in *A Farewell to Arms*,' *Modern Fiction Studies*, VII (Summer, 1961), 169.
66. Light 169.
67. E.M. Halliday, 'Hemingway's Ambiguity : Symbolism and Irony,' *American Literature*, XXVIII (March, 1966), 15.
68. Baker, Hemingway; *The Writer as Artist* (Princeton, 1956), 116.
69. Baker 116.
70. Baker 116.

4

For Whom the Bell Tolls

FOR WHOM the Bell Tolls was published in 1940; precisely speaking, it came out on October 21, 1940, and it took Hemingway nearly eighteen months, from March 1939 to September 1940, to complete the writing of this novel. In a sense, Hemingway was always close to Spain, chiefly for its bull-fighting, its earthiness, its primitivism, and when the Civil War between the Republicans or Loyalists on the one hand and the Fascists on the other broke out there is July 1936, with the foreign powers taking sides in this bloody political turmoil, Hemingway just could not do without getting increasingly involved in it to help the anti-Fascist forces there. In this connection he first visited Spain in February 1937 and stayed there till May of the same year; his second visit to this country covered a period of nearly six months from August 1937 to January 1938; he visited Spain for the third time in March 1938 and continued to be there till May 1938, but when he went to Spain once again in September 1938, he could very well see the collapse of the anti-Fascist forces there. It was only six months later that he started writing the novel sometime in March 1939. It is not unnatural that *For Whom the Bell Tolls* could have been written as a political novel, or as an exercise in political propaganda; instead, it is very much a work of art. In fact, *For Whom the Bell Tolls* is as much a work of art at Gustav Regler's novel, *The Great Crusade,* Ralph Bate's novel, *The Oliver Field,* and Andre Malraux's novel, *L'Espoir,* are the acclaimed works of art.[1]

The critical response to this novel has been mixed in nature.

Carlos Baker says that Hemingway selected 'the early summer of 1937 as the time of Jordan's action'[2] for very important reasons, that he 'wanted a period deep enough into the war so that the possibility of Republican defeat could be a meaningful psychological force,'[3] that 'the time must also be far enough removed from the end of the war so that some of his people could still believe in a Republican victory,'[4] and that 'as a study in doom, the novel must early isolate and dramatize these adverse powers and power-failures which would ultimately combine to defeat the Spanish Republic.'[5] He states further that 'if *For Whom the Bell Tolls* is a kind of epic, it is above all a tragic epic'[6] and that 'rich as it is in symbolic extensions, it is somewhere near a synecdochist's triumph.'[7] In his very illuminating essay entitled, "Mechanized Doom": Ernest Hemingway and the American View of the Spanish Civil War, Allen Guttmann observes that the central issue in *For Whom the Bell Tolls* is the symbolic opposition between man and machine and that for Hemingway 'the Spanish Civil War was, among other things, a struggle waged by men close to the earth and to the values of a primitive society against men who had turned away from the earth, men who had turned to the machine and to the antithetical values of an aggressive and destructive mechanical order.'[8]

In his comments on the present novel, Lionel Trilling says that it contains the grains of both success and failure. He says that 'Here, we feel at once, is a restored Hemingway writing to the top of his bent'[9] and that this novel is 'flexible enough, or ambiguous enough, to allow Hemingway a more varied notion of life than he has ever before achieved.'[10] And though he calls *For Whom the Bell Tolls* a 'novel of arrogant political will'[11] and points to 'the essential inner dullness'[12] of Robert Jordan, he maintains that 'from the beginning of the novel to the end, one has the happy sense of the author's unremitting and successful poetic effort.'[13] In his concluding observation about the present novel we find him stating that the 'major movement of the novel is...a failure, and a failure the more to be regretted because it has so many of the elements of great success.'[14] In its turn, Alvah C. Bessie's review of *For Whom the Bell Tolls* is downright damaging in nature. Although Bessie admits that this novel is indeed 'an artistic triumph'[15] in so far as the evocation of moods and the crystallization of certain fundamental human emotions are concerned, yet he says:

> Many expected that Hemingway's experience in Spain would so inflame his heart and his talents, that his long-announced novel of that war would be both his finest achievement and 'the' novel about Spain. It is not. It is his finest achievement only in the sense that he has now perfected his extraordinary technical facility and touched some moments of action with a fictional suspense that is literally unbearable. But depth of understanding there is none; breadth of conception is heart-breakingly lacking; there is no searching, no probing, no grappling with the truths of human life that is more than superficial.[16]

And, as he puts it, 'an astounding thing has happened, that anyone who was even remotely concerned with Spain will find almost incredible: Hemingway has treated that war (in an essential way) exactly as he treated the First World War in *A Farewell to Arms.*'[17] He further observes:

> It must be clearly stated that Hemingway's position in this novel is unequivocally on the side of the Spanish people; there can be no question of his defection from that cause. It is, however, a tragic fact that the cause of Spain does not, in any essential way, figure as a motivating power, a driving, emotional, passional force in this story.[18]

Bessie argues over again and again to stress the point that this novel stands for a betrayal of 'those talents'[19] that Hemingway had acquired, developed and perfected over a number of years.

Nevertheless, all appraisals of *For Whom the Bell Tolls* take us to the basic fact that this novel does have its own network of symbolism and that its symbols and images have to be explored and understood carefully in order to be able to get at its real significance.

The action in this novel covers a span of seventy-two hours only, and Hemingway renders all his experiences of Spain, its people, and of the war going on there within this very time-frame. And the protagonist of the novel, Robert Jordan, too has to live his life within this very time-limit. Nevertheless, this novel deals as much with the past of its characters as with their present. It is, then, quite natural that the plot of this novel is more complex than and different from the plots of Hemingway's other novels.

II

The first thing that attracts our attention in *For Whom the Bell Tolls* is the epigraph which has been taken from one of John Donne's meditations and which gives the book its title:

> No man is an *Iland,* intire of it selfe; every man is a peace of the *Continent,* a part of the *maine;* if a *Clod* bee washed away by the *Sea, Europe* is the lesse, as well as if a *Promontorie* were, as well as if a *Mannor* of thy *friends,* or of *thine owne* were; any mans *death* diminishes *me,* because I am involved in *Mankinde;* And therefore, never send to know for whom the *bell* tolls; It tolls for *thee.* John Donne[20]

Hemingway, says Allen Guttmann in his essay entitled "Mechanized Doom:" Ernest Hemingway and the American View of the Spanish Civil War,' 'uses this epigraph as a statement of the theme of brotherhood, of human solidarity, of the involvement of all men in a common humanity.'[21] However, both A.C. Bessie and Lionel Trilling have to say something different in this regard. Bessie comments that the author of *the Bell* does not convince us, with this novel, that "any mans death diminishes me, because I am involved in Mankinde."[22] Trilling too finds an appreciable gap between Hemingway's intention and his actual performance:

> For Donne, death is the appaling negation and therefore the teacher of the ego. For Hemingway, death is the ego's final expression and the perfect protector of the personality. It is a sentimental error from which Donne

> was saved by his great power of mind.... Hemingway, so much at the service of the cult of experience, debars himself from what Donne learned from his contemplation of death. As a consequence, it is the isolation of the individual ego in its search for experience that Hemingway celebrates in this novel that announces as its theme the community of men.[23]

Mark Schorer sums up this discrepancy in his own way when he says that in spite of 'the omnious premium which the title seems to place on individuality, the real theme of this book is the relative unimportance of individuality and the superb importance of the political whole.'[24] Notwithstanding this serious flaw about the title of the novel and keeping it in view, we may proceed to undertake a consideration of the symbols and images that we get in the present novel.

The first important symbol that we encounter in *For Whom the Bell Tolls* is the bridge which Robert Jordan, along with his companions, has to blow up; it is the centre of all attention, the hub of all activities, in the novel. Not unnaturally, the word 'bridge' finds mention for two hundred ninety-four times in the novel. In Chapter I alone, it appears for thirty-two times. Thinking of this bridge which he has to blow up with explosives, Robert Jordan tells himself:

> And that is not the way to think,... and there is not you, and there are no people that things must not happen to. Neither you nor this old man is anything. You are instruments to do your duty. There are necessary orders that are no fault of yours and there is a bridge and that bridge can be the point on which the future of the human race can turn, as it can turn on everything that happens in this war. You have only one thing to do and you must do it.[25]

And, in a way, Pilar reciprocates Jordan's attitude towards the bridge when she says; 'I am for the Republic.... And the Republic is the bridge.'[26] This bridge is not merely strategically vital both for the Republicans and the Fascists in the Civil War; it is also important for mankind as a whole, for its blowing up would signify the victory of the Republican cause and the undoing of Fascism at one and the same time. Speaking in physical terms, the destruction of this bridge would result in a severe dislocation of the movement and demoralization of the Fascist forces. Judged from this point of view, the bridge may be looked upon as a symbol of freedom, of hope for the future of the human race itself. It is this microcosm-macrocosm dimension of the bridge that lends it its real significance.

Although we are aware of the importance of this bridge right from the beginning of the novel, we first get a description of it only in Chapter III of the book:

> They came down the last two hundred yards, moving carefully from tree to tree, in the shadows and now, through the last pines of the steep hillside, the bridge was only fifty yards away. The late afternoon sun that still came over the brown shoulder of the mountain showed the bridge dark against the steep emptiness of the gorge. It was a steel bridge of a single span and there was a sentry box at each end. It was wide enough for two motor-cars to pass, and it spanned, in solidflung metal grace, a deep gorge at the bottom of which, far below, a brook leaped in white water through rocks and boulders down to the mainstream of the pass.[27]

Robert Jordan and his men inspect this bridge from as close a distance as they could do so in the given situation, for it is the Fascists who control and guard it in order to be able to keep the Madrid-Valencia road open for the desired movement of their troops and mechanized weapons. 'Just as the lighthouse,' says Allen Guttmann in his essay entitled, "Mechanized Doom:" Ernest Hemingway and the American View of the Spanish Civil War, 'dominates the action of Virginia Woolf's novel, so the bridge controls and unifies the action of Hemingway's. In one sense, it is the center of a series of concentric circles; in another, it is the point toward which the elements of the plot coverage.'[28] Almost all the characters in the novel are, in one way or another, involved with the bridge, and while the Republicans are determined to blow it up, the Fascists are also equally duty-bound to protect it for strategic reasons. Robert Jordan is under orders to blow up the bridge, and he enlists the support of Pablo and his people to be able to complete his assignment. It is towards this end that while on the one hand he is so very confident of getting co-operation and assistance from such persons of Pablo's band as Anselmo, Fernando, Primitivo, Eladio, Agustin, Andrés, Pilar and Maria, he is rather uncertain about Rafael and sorely suspicious of Pablo.

Robert Jordan, as he tells Maria, is not a communist, but an 'anti-Fascist.'[29] By profession, he is an instructor in Spanish at the University of Montana; he is an American, and so an expatriate, and yet he has been in Spain for over ten years before the outbreak of the Civil War in this country. He loves Spain, and tells Pilar: 'there are no other countries like Spain.'[30] He does also love the people of Spain, for he thinks: 'They are wonderful when they are good.... There is no people like them when they are good and when they go bad there is no people that is worse.'[31] Robert Jordan gives no importance to what may happen to him; he can, as General Golz puts it, "blow bridges very well,"[32] and he makes his position very clear to Pablo when he tells him:

> 'I come only for my duty.... I come under orders from those who are conducting the war. If I ask you to help me, you can refuse and I will find others who will help me. I have not even asked you for help yet. I have to do what I am ordered to do and I can promise you of its importance. That I am a foreigner is not my fault. I would rather have been born here.'[33]

It is quite understandable that he thinks: 'My obligation is the bridge, and to fulfil that I must take no useless risk of myself until I complete that duty.'[34] He tells himself: 'He would not think himself into defeatism. The first thing was to win the war,'[35] and he is determined to drop that bridge into the gorge 'like a broken bird-cage.'[36] It is with this objective in view that even though he is not a communist, he has volunteered himself for work under the communist leadership. He tells himself:

> He fought now in this war because it had started in a country that he loved and he believed in the Republic and that if it were destroyed life would be unbearable for all those people who believed in it. He was under Communist discipline for the duration of the war. Here in Spain the Communists offered the best discipline and the soundest and sanest for the prosecution of the war. He accepted their discipline for the duration of the war because, in the conduct of the war, they were the only party whose programme and whose discipline he could respect.[37]

It is with this conviction, this determination, this firm faith in discipline that he succeeds in blowing up the bridge. And though he is seriously wounded and left alone among the pine-trees, he does have the immense satisfaction of having completed his task. He speaks to himself; 'I have fought for what I believed in for a year now. If we win here we will win everywhere. The world is a fine place and worth the fighting for and I hate very much to leave it.'[38]

Moreover, it is also important to note that Robert Jordan is not just a teacher of Spanish and a lover of Spain, but also a writer, and that he proposes to write a book on Spain when he is free. Quite understandably, he looks upon Fascism as 'the death of art'[39] and also as 'the death of everything that the artist values and needs.'[40] Writing about Robert Jordan, Carlos Baker says:

> Working efficiently as a dynamiter with the Republican guerrillas, loving Spain, hating Fascism, sympathizing with the people who have been and are being betrayed, Jordan still manages to be temperate without being at all tepid. His brain is neither dominated nor deceived by the propagandistic. He remains the free man, the man not taken in, the man doing the necessary job but also making the necessary mental reservations.[41]

And he goes on to say: 'Robert Jordan is capable of working for a cause without allowing its heretical errors to eat their way like acid into his deeper convictions.'[42]

'A short and solid old man in a black peasant's smock,'[43] Anselmo belongs to Barco de Avila and is sixty-eight years of age. By his very faith and temperament, he is against all human killings. He tells Robert Jordan: 'To me it is a sin to kill a man,'[44] and goes on to say: 'To take the life of another is very grave.'[45] And yet, he assures Robert Jordan of his assistance when he tells him: 'I will do that to which I am assigned.'[46] He knows that killing is unavoidable in war, and still he spurns the very idea of killing a human being. Nevertheless, he is terribly angry with the Fascists and wants to 'take away their planes, their automatic weapons, their tanks, their artillery, and teach them dignity.'[47] Anselmo is 'a Christian'[48] and of the native Spaniards in the novel, 'none better exemplifies the right human norm than Anselmo.'[49] It is quite in keeping with his character that he dies in the process of blowing the bridge.

Agustin, Fernando, Eladio, Primitivo and Andrés—they are all ready to fight for the cause of the Republic and to die for it; in fact, Eladio and Fernando die in the course of demolition of the bridge. And Agustin and Andres do whatever they could to assist Robert Jordan in the accomplishment of his task. Fernando, says J.W. Beach, is 'a stiff and pedantic person, but the soul of loyalty and courage;'[50] he is 'brave and firm, and can be relied on to perform whatever duty requires.'[51] Agustin, no doubt, is a crude and rough-mouthed person, but he does have the grains of understanding in him to tell Pilar: 'To make war all you need is intelligence. But to win you need talent and material.'[52]

Pablo and Rafael form a separate group altogether. Rafael, says Anselmo, 'catches rabbits.... He is a gipsy. So if he catches rabbits he says it is foxes. If he catches a fox he would say it was an elephant.'[53] Pilar is of the view that 'the mind of the gipsy is corrupt.'[54] Rafael is an irresponsible person, and Robert Jordan is disgusted with him because, instead of standing guard on his post, he leaves it to catch rabbits. It is in this context that Jordan calls him 'worthless.'[55] And yet he needs him and keeps him in his company. Carlos Baker speaks of Rafael's 'irresponsible paganism,'[56] and observes that if General Golz is 'not free enough to prosecute a war successfully, then the Rafaels of the Republican side are too free and too irresponsible'[57] to realize the seriousness of the situation.

Pablo is the 'boss'[58] of his band; he is a strong man; he is an anti-Fascist and a Republican, and yet he is not inclined to lend help to Robert Jordan, chiefly because if any attempt is made to blow up the bridge, he and his band would be hunted out of the mountains. Jordan notices a sadness on his face, a sadness people 'get before they quit or before they betray,'[59] a sadness that 'comes before the sell-out.'[60] In his turn, Pablo looks upon Robert Jordan as a foreigner, and rebukes him when he tells him: 'What right have you, a foreigner, to come to me and tell me what I must do.'[61] He makes it very clear to Jordan that he is not going to co-operate with him in his venture. He says: 'I do not go for the bridge.... Neither me nor my people.'[62] At the beginning of the movement and earlier also, Pablo was virile, energetic, manly and dynamic, but now he is 'a ruin,'[63] 'a garbage of what he once was.'[64] As Pilar puts it, he has been 'rendered useless by his fear and his disinclination to action.'[65] Pablo first tries to hamper Jordan's action and then even steals some of his dynamite, detonators and other explosives which he throws away at will, but later he joins Jordan's group only to kill his newly-recruited men and to leave the handicapped and injured American all by himself to languish among the pine trees. In his essay entitled, 'Mechanized Doom:' Ernest Hemingway and the American View of the Spanish Civil War,' Allen Guttmann observes that Hemingway's 'portrayal of Pablo indicates that the book is not a naive affirmation of the Noble Savage.'[66] And Carlos Baker comments that Pablo is not merely 'a specific Judas'[67] but also 'a recognizable symbol for the general canker of defeatism, gnawing the tissues of Republican morale from within, and leading to the larger betrayal.'[68]

Almost throughout the novel, Pilar is called the woman of Pablo or the '*mujer* of Pablo;'[69] she is even debunked by some of her own people as the 'whore of whores,'[70] for she has been staying with Pablo without being his wife, just as earlier she had lived with three of the worst-paid matadors of her country. She is a primitive woman; she may be 'barbarous,'[71] but she is hardy and brave, and is whole-heartedly committed to the Republican cause. She tells Robert Jordan: 'I put great illusion in the Republic. I believe firmly in the Republic and I have faith. I believe in it with fervour as those who have religious faith believe in the mysteries.'[72] She has, as Rafael informs Robert Jordan, 'gipsy blood'[73] in her, and, what is more, she is said to be gifted with supersensory powers. She is indeed all out for the American dynamiter, and does everything within her powers or reach to protect and help him. Pilar is also a good story-teller, for she narrates the story of the massacre of the Fascists in a highly engaging manner.[74] And, obviously enough, it is she who encourages both Robert Jordan and Maria to move so very close to each other. Pablo's woman, says J.W. Beach, is a 'formidable master of invective, jealous and passionate, but absolutely devoted to a leader she can trust, and the most tough and resolute of all the comrades.'[75] In his essay entitled "Mechanized Doom:" Ernest Hemingway and the American View of the Spanish Civil War, Allen Guttmann comments that Pilar is 'a kind of Iberian Earth-Mother who is proud that the world itself moved during her love-making who had lived nine years with three of the worst-paid matadors in the world, who reminds us again and again of the love-making and bull-fighting that represent Spain as it should have been.'[76] In his turn, Carlos Baker observes that even though Pilar is 'as tough as an old eagle...the heart still beats for humankind even when the head coldly admits the need for violent activity against the enemy.'[77]

Maria is a young girl, eighteen years of age, with a beautiful face, and she has been living with the Pablo band in the cave up on the mountain ever since her escape from the captivity of the Fascists. She is out and out a Republican, and a terrible anti-Fascist: her father was the Mayor of his village and a staunch Republican, whom the Fascists had shot dead. The Fascists capture, torture and rape Maria, and it is no less unfortunate that they get her hair regularly shaved in the Valladolid prison. By the time Robert Jordan comes to Pablo, her hair has grown only a little. That is why, fondly though, she is at times also addressed as 'little cropped head.'[78] The cutting of Maria's hair is a symbol of her loss of normal womanhood or girlhood, just as its 'growing-out indicates her gradual return to balance and health.'[79] It is partly on account of her proximity to and liking for Robert Jordan and partly because of Pilar's encouragement that Maria and the American dynamiter move very close to each other. In fact, Maria dreams of becoming Robert Jordan's wife and of going to Madrid and other places with him, though, as things go, she does not succeed in realizing her dreams. Maria may or may not be the 'perfect sexual creature of the private Hemingway mythology,'[80] but, as Pilar knows, it is Jordan's love for her that can erase 'the psychological scars'[81] the Fascists have left on her memory. 'The significance of Maria,' says Carlos Baker, 'when she is seen in the light of such other heroines as Catherine Barkley, Marie Morgan, and even Dorothy Bridges, is finally symbolic. In the lonely alien region of the Guadarramas, she comes to stand as the image of 'home.'[82]

It is these people—Robert Jordan, Anselmo, Fernando, Agustin, Primitivo, Eladio, Andrés, Pilar, Maria, and also Pablo and Rafael, if only reluctantly—who blow up the bridge or contribute, either directly or indirectly, to its demolition. 'The bridge,' says Robert Jordan, 'is a part of the plan to win the war,'[83] and he believes that if the bridge is demolished, the Republicans can capture Segovia, the capital of a province. The bridge is at last blown up, and towards the end of the novel we do see the steel bridge rendered all useless for traffic:

> ...there was a cracking roar and the middle of the bridge rose up in the air like a wave breaking and he [Robert Jordan] felt the blast from the explosion roll back against him as he dived on to his face in the pebbly gully with his hands holding tight over his head. His face was down against the pebbles as the bridge settled where it had risen and the familiar yellow smell of it rolled over him in acrid smoke and then it commenced to rain pieces of steel.[84]

Robert Jordan succeeds in performing his assigned duty. However, it is more as a symbol than anything else that this bridge pervades the novel. The form of the novel, says Carlos Baker, is 'that of a series of concentric circles with the all-important bridge in the middle.'[85] And he goes on to say: 'His [Robert Jordan's] bridge is at the center of the history of holding actions; and although his problem is small in scale, it is so conceived and projected as to suggest a struggle of epical dimensions.'[86]

As a symbol, the bridge in *For Whom the Bell Tolls* does indeed have its own ubiquitous importance and profound significance, but at the same time, it does also raise certain issues that have their own symbolic implications. The bridge is made of steel and such other things, of which tanks, armoured vehicles and other weapons are made, while Spain and its people, in their own right, stand for Nature, for the earth, for primitivism itself. This brings us to the essential conflict between man and machine, between Nature and the technological civilization, as it is projected in the novel. It is indeed very significant that *For Whom the Bell Tolls* begins and ends with 'the pine-needle floor of the forest,'[87] that from time to time it reverberates with the thunderous roar of the aeroplanes, that the Fascist aircraft bomb and destroy EI Sordo and his band, and that Pablo and his people look at them, all awe-struck and terror-stricken, viewing them as the very agents of disaster and death. Even Robert Jordan, an American, does not remain unaffected by them. As he and Anselmo are inspecting the bridge from a reasonably safe distance, they hear two kinds of noise, the first kind coming from the stream or Nature, the second from the aeroplanes or machine:

> From the gorge came the noise of the stream in the boulders. Then through this noise came another noise, a steady, racketing drone and they saw the sentry looking up, his knitted cap slanted back, and turning their heads and looking up they saw, high in the evening sky, three monoplanes in V formation, showing minute and silvery at that height where there still was sun, passing

> unbelievably quickly across the sky, their motors now throbbing steadily.[88]

It is quite natural that these flying craft compel Robert Jordan to think of them and of future:

> The bombers were high now in fast, ugly arrow-heads beating the sky apart with the noise of their motors. They are shaped like sharks, Robert Jordan thought, the wide-finned, sharp-nosed sharks of the Gulf Stream. But these, wide-finned in silver, roaring, the light mist of their propellers in the sun, these do not move like sharks. They move like nothing there has ever been. They move like mechanized doom.[89]

'The mountain-sanctuary', observes Carlos Baker, '...is now shown to be open to invasion and destruction by the Fascist bombers, which the artist carefully establishes as symbols of the power of evil.'[90] And in his essay entitled, "Mechanized Doom:" Ernest Hemingway and the American View of the Spanish Civil War, Allen Guttmann says that it is perfectly natural that 'bombing planes and armored tanks should become...symbols for the enemy'[91] and that these symbols are limited for the simple and obvious reason that they 'corresponded to the historical situation.'[92] Significantly enough, Pilar calls these aeroplanes 'the bad luck bird'[93] in her own native idiom.

It is quite meaningful that most of these aeroplanes come in threes or in the formations of three. It is Robert Jordan who makes a pointed note of this number:

> Lying on his back, he saw them, a Fascist patrol of three Fiats, tiny, bright, fast-moving across the mountain sky, headed in the direction from which Anselmo and he had come yesterday. The three passed and then came nine more, flying much higher in the minute, pointed formations of threes, threes, and threes.[94]

Interestingly enough, while bombing El Sordo's hideout, these planes come back thrice:

> The planes came back three times and bombed the hilltop but no one on the hilltop knew it. Then the planes machine-gunned the hilltop and went away. As they dived

> on the hill for the last time with their machine guns hammering, the first plane pulled up and winged over and then each plane did the same and they moved from echelon to V-formation and went away into the sky in the direction of Segovia.[95]

Now, speaking traditionally or numerologically, three is a magical or mysterious number, a number supposed to have supernatural or occult associations. In this connection Carlos Baker comments:

> Hemingway's linking of the modern bombers with the ancient magic-symbol of number three greatly enhances the emotional effectiveness of the plane-passage. The old epics and the great dramatic tragedies could employ supernatural agents in the full expectation that they would intensify the emotions of pity and terror in the spectator. The rise of naturalism, and the partial decay of superstition, denied the tragic artist direct across to one of his most evocative instruments. Yet within the shadowy subconscious, the perennial human capacity for fear and awe remained to be touched by any artist who could empower new symbols with old terrors.[96]

It is really highly ironic that while the primitive people of Spain speak and think in terms of 'crows,'[97] 'hawks,'[98] 'rabbits,'[99] 'foxes,'[100] 'elephants,'[101] and 'horses,'[102] the Fascists in Spain take recourse to machines and mechanized war.

In spite of his being an American and his education, Robert Jordan, essentially speaking, belongs to Spain and is an inalienable part of Spain's primitivism. And that is why, he loves and enjoys the charms and wonder and glory of Nature:

> He loved this hour of the day always and now he watched it; feeling it grey within him, as though he were a part of the slow lightening that comes before the rising of the sun; when solid things darken and space lightens and the lights that have shone in the night go yellow and then fade as the day comes.[103]

However, as he is lying behind the pine tree, the serenity and calm of Nature are rudely disturbed by the pounding of the bombs:

> He lay there behind the pine tree, with the sub-machine gun across his left forearm, and he never looked at the sentry box again until, long after it seemed that it was never coming, that nothing could happen on such a lovely late May morning, he heard the sudden, clustered, thudding of the bombs.[104]

The bull-fight too,[105] to which frequent references are made in the present novel, stands for the earthiness, the manliness, the primitive heroism of the Spanish people. The young boy, Joaquin, comes out with the characteristic Spanish sentiment when he tells Pilar: "We have seen much worse things and more dangerous than the bulls. It is clear no bull is as dangerous as a machine gun."[106] In fact, as Carlos Baker puts it, *For Whom the Bell Tolls* 'follows an architectural plan comparable to that of a Spanish bull-ring, which is constructed in a series of concentric circles, so arranged that from any point one can watch the action taking place at the centre.'[107]

Spain, observes Allen Guttmann in his essay entitled "Mechanized Doom:" Ernest Hemingway and the American View of the Spanish Civil War is 'an elemental symbiosis of man and nature.'[108] And it is this 'symbiosis of man and nature' that is rudely shaken and sought to be destroyed by the Fascist bombers and tanks.

Besides these symbols of the bridge, Nature, the bombers and tanks, the mystical number three and the bull-ring or bull-fight in *For Whom the Bell Tolls*, in it we do also come across a few other symbols and images of appreciable relevance and importance. The wheel is one such symbol in the novel. In the tense quiet of the evening, preceding the morning when the bridge has to be blown up as scheduled, Robert Jordan, sitting inside Pablo's cave, speculates on the prospects of his action, and it is in this context that he thinks of the wheel:

> It was like a merry-go-ground, Robert Jordan thought. Not a merry-go-round that travels fast and with a calliope for music, and the children ride on cows with gilded horns, and there are rings to catch with sticks, and there is the blue, gas-flare-lit early dark of the Avenue du

> Maine, with fried fish sold from the next stall, and a wheel of fortune turning with the leather flaps slapping against the posts of the unnumbered compartments, and the packages of lump sugar piled in pyramids for prizes. No, it is not that kind of a merry-go-round: although the people are waiting, like the men in caps and the women in knitted sweaters, their heads bare in the gaslight and their hair shining, who stand in front of the wheel of fortune as it spins. Yes, those are the people. But this is another wheel. This is like a wheel that goes up and around.[109]

Robert Jordan is not really thinking of the 'merry-go-round' wheel or of the 'wheel of fortune;' at the moment, since he is very much disturbed by Pablo's attitude of hostility, he is thinking of yet another kind of wheel:

> It has been around twice now. It is a vast wheel, set at an angle, and each time it goes around and then is back to where it starts. One side is higher than the other and the sweep it makes lifts you back and down to where you started. There are no prizes either, he thought, and no one would choose to ride this wheel. You ride it each time and make the turn with no intention ever to have mounted. There is only one turn; one large, elliptical, rising and falling turn and you are back where you have started. We are back again now, he thought, and nothing is settled.[110]

However, in spite of uncertainties and the danger of betrayal, Robert Jordan musters plenty of courage and boldness so as to keep himself off from this wheel:

> There will be Pablo or there will be no Pablo. I care nothing about it either way. But I am not going to get on that wheel again. Twice I have been on that wheel and twice it has gone around and come back to where it started and I am taking no more rides on it.[111]

We may call it, for want of a better term, the 'wheel of human conflict;'[112] but whatever it is or may be, the turn of this wheel has 'tragic implications.'[113] In fact, the wheel symbolizes 'the wheel-like turn of Spain's tragedy'[114] and suggests that 'after all the agony and all the blood nothing should be settled, and that Spain should be back where it began, in a medieval situation.'[115]

The two other symbols that have their bearing on the nature of Communism in relation to the Spanish Republican movement, are Velazquez 63 and Gaylordś. As Robert Jordan thinks of them inside Pablo's cave on the high slopes of the Sierra de Guadarramas amidst the cluster of pine trees, several things come to his mind:

> At either of those places you felt that you were taking part in a crusade. That was the only word for it although it was a word that had been so worn and abused that it no longer gave its true meaning. You felt, in spite of all bureaucracy and inefficiency and party strife, something that was like the feeling you expected to have and did not have when you made your first communion. It was a feeling of consecration to a duty toward all of the oppressed of the world would be as difficult and embarrassing to speak about as religious experience and yet it was authentic as the feeling you had when you heard Bach or stood in Chartres Cathedral or the Cathedral at Léon and saw the light coming through the great windows; or when saw Mantegna and Greco and Brueghel in the Prado.[116]

No doubt, Velazquez 63 and Gaylordś, remembers Robert Jordan, do have something that is common to each other, and yet he is quite aware of the difference between the two kinds of Communism that are taught and practised at these two places or institutions. Velazquez 63, the headquarters of International Brigade in Madrid, preaches and practises a kind of Communism that is 'puritanical,'[117] 'religious'[118] in spirit; here, it is like being a member of a religious order.[119] On the other hand, Gaylordś is a place where 'you met famous peasant and worker Spanish commanders who had sprung to arms from the people at the start of the war without any previous military training and found that many of them spoke Russian;'[120] it is the place 'you needed to complete your education;'[121] it is the place that seemed indecently luxurious and corrupt,[122] and it is the place which believes that 'there was always lying in a war.'[123] it is chiefly because of Gaylordś and its people, such as André Marty and others, that the Republican movement in Spain suffers and flounders. Like Robert Jordan, Hemingway too was not a Communist; he was only an anti-Fascist, and all that he wants to suggest through these two symbols is that while some of the Communists in Spain were idealistic and sincere people, a large majority of them were deceitful, irresponsible and cynical ones, not at all worthy of trust.

In addition to all these symbols in *For Whom the Bell Tolls*, it is the odour image and the term *nada* in the novel that attract our attention. This novel is pervaded by a large variety of odours. The 'odours of different herbs,'[124] 'the odour of pine needles,'[125] the 'smell of the mob,'[126] the smell of 'spilled wine and vomit,'[127] the 'smell of the roots and the earth,'[128] the 'odours of the cave,'[129] the 'odour of death'[130] the 'odour of the onion,'[131] the 'smell of the leggings and the shirts'[132] and the 'smell of the horses'[133] are cases in point. And it is not without significance that Pilar tells Robert Jordan about the three blended odours of the smell of death: 'In this sack will be contained the essence of it all, both the dead earth and the dead stalks of the flowers and their rotted blooms and the smell that is both the death and birth of man.'[134] In his turn, Robert Jordan remembers and thinks of several odours:

> The night was clear and his head felt as clear and cold as the air. He smelled the odour of the pine boughs under him, the piny smell of the crushed needles, and the sharper odour of the resinous sap from the cut limbs. Pilar, he thought. Pilar and the smell of death. This is the smell I love. This and fresh-cut clover, the crushed sage as you ride after cattle, wood-smoke, and the burning leaves of autumn. That must be the odour of nostalgia, the smell of the smoke from the piles of raked leaves burning in the streets in the fall in Missoula. Which would you rather smell? Sweet grass the Indians used in their baskets? Smoked leather? The odour of the ground in the spring after rain? The smell of the sea as you walk

> through the gorse on a headland in Galicia? Or the wind from the land as you come in toward Cuba in the dark? That was the odour of the cactus flowers, mimosa, and the sea-grape shrubs. Or would you rather smell frying bacon in the morning when you are hungry? Or coffee in the morning? Or a Jonathan apple as you bite into it? Or a cider mill in the grinding, or bread fresh from the oven?[135]

Besides being an authentic index to Hemingway's olfactory sensitivity, these odours are symbolic in the sense that they present a contrast between the idyllic locale of Pablo's cave and the tragedy that is to befall Robert Jordan, some of Pablo's men, and Spain itself.

The term *nada*, meaning 'nothing,' 'nothing more,' or 'nothingness,' has been used for about eleven times in *For Whom the Bell Tolls*. This term is spoken or used by the primitive but militant people of Spain, that Anselmo, Pilar and such others of Pablo's group are, and as such there is hardly anything philosophical about it. And yet, this term points to something sinister that is to invade, disturb and perhaps destroy the scene of action among the high slopes of the Sierra de Guadarramas, which do strike us as a clean, well-lighted place where the weather is cold and the air clear.

III

The symbols that we come across in *For Whom the Bell Tolls* do indeed highlight the conflict between Republicanism and Fascism, but at the same time they do also bring out the contrast between Nature and science, between the primitive way of life and the technological civilization. And it is in keeping with this very theme of contrast that we find Hemingway making use of images in the present novel.

A large number of images in *For Whom the Bell Tolls* take us straight on to Nature. Pablo's camp or cave, high up on the mountain, is quite safe and 'as well hidden as a bear's den.'[136] Robert Jordan and Pilar fondly look upon Maria as 'a very pleasant rabbit;'[137] Jordan loves stroking Maria 'like a kitten;'[138]

Maria moves awkwardly as a colt[139] does, but 'with that some grace as of a young animal;'[140] her hair is 'the golden brown of a grain field that has been burned dark in the sun,'[141] and 'if anyone touched her she would shiver like a wet dog.'[142] Pablo, his associates say, has, in the course of the movement, killed more people than 'the cholera..., the typhoid fever...and the bubonic plague'[143] could kill; Robert Jordan looks at Pablo 'with his mouth closed so that his lips made a tight line, like the mouth of a fish;'[144] he watches Pablo's' 'eyes narrow, as a cat's pupils close to vertical slits in a strong light,'[145] and Agustin curses Pablo, 'speaking slowly, clearly, bitterly, and contemptuously and cursing as steadily as though he were dumping manure on a field, lifting it with a dung fork out of a wagon.'[146] Robert Jordan thinks that Pilar is 'like a mountain;'[147] Maria imagines that Pilar looks 'like a dark bundle...; black against the brown of the tree trunk;'[148] Robert Jordan think that plan spreads herself out 'as a cobra's hood spreads,'[149] and he does also surmise that the boy, Joaquin, and Maria are growing 'like young trees.'[150]

It hardly requires explaining that all these images are, in a way, Hemingway's points to the basic earthiness of the Spanish people.

It is indeed true that Hemingway does also employ images which he borrows from the field of science. Speaking of Pilar's curses, Hemingway observes that 'the woman started to curse in a flood of obscene invective that rolled over and around him like the hot white water splashing down from the sudden eruption of a geyser.'[151] As Anselmo gulps down whisky, while he is in a state of depression, he gets warmed up and feels that it is 'as good a thing for his spirit as a saline injection is for a man who has suffered a great haemorrhage.'[152] With Pablo's return to the camp and his promise to Robert Jordan to lend him his help in the demolition of the bridge, the American dynamiter feels 'confidence rising in him as a tyre begins to fill with air from a slow pump.'[153] The Russians, comments an officer, 'are purging more than the Epsom salts in this epoch.'[154] And Robert Jordan is said to be working as fast and skilfully for the demolition of the bridge as 'a surgeon works'[155] with his tolls on the operation table.

These science-related images are found in the novel mostly in the form of authorial comments, and they refer to the technological civilization of the present-day world.

Hemingway does also offer religious images in *For Whom the Bell Tolls*. Telling us about the bull-fighter, Finito, Pilar says that 'he would not look up at the bull's head, which was shrouded in a purple cloth as the images of the saints are covered in church.'[156] And in his turn, as Anselmo goes on with his prayer among the pine trees, he sees 'the light coming through the tree trunks in patches as it comes through the columns of a cathedral.'[157]

However, it is really interesting to find even scientific objects being presented in *For Whom the Bell Tolls* in terms of animals, birds and marine species. The train engine falling on to its side is 'like a great wounded animal.'[158] Robert Jordan packs his explosives 'as carefully as he had packed his collection of wild bird eggs when he was a boy,'[159] and he counts 'fifteen Fiats in echelon of echelons like a wild-goose flight of the V-shaped three.'[160] The shadows of the Heinkels move over the land 'as the shadows of sharks pass over a sandy floor of the ocean,'[161] and the bombers, Robert Jordan tells himself, are the 'wide-finned, sharp-nosed sharks of the Gulf Stream.'[162]

It is so very easy to see that Hemingway draws his symbols and images from a variety of sources, and he exploits his own experiences of war and fishing and hunting for their functional employment in *For Whom the Bell Tolls*.

IV

In his comments on *For Whom the Bell Tolls*, Carlos Baker identifies the 'elements of the epic manner'[163] that Hemingway adapts to his needs in this novel, and in this connection observes:

> Despite the obvious gap between Spain and Ilium, the student of the epic may find part of his answer in considering the Homeric parallel. A primitive setting,

> simple food and wine, the care and use of weapons, the sense of imminent danger, the emphasis on masculine prowess, the presence of varying degrees of courage and cowardice, the rude barbarisms on both sides, the operation of certain religious and magical superstitions, the warrior codes—these, surely, are common ties between the two sets of protagonists. Jordan is not to be scorned as the type of Achilles, and one can recoginze in Pablo the rude outlines of a debased and sulking Ajax. Pilar the gypsy, though she reads the lifeline in Jordan's palm instead of consulting the shape and colour of animal entrails, makes the consciousness of the supernatural an operative factor.[164]

Moreover, Baker does also refer to 'the intentionally heightened language'[165] that Hemingway adopts in the present novel.

We may or may not accept *For Whom the Bell Tolls* as an epic of sorts, but we can hardly be unmindful of the novel's shortcomings. Pilar's narration of the story of the massacre of the Fascists in Chapter 10 of the novel does not seem to be quite justified, even though it seeks to glorify Pablo who is now merely a cowardly ghost of his former brave and determined self. Similarly, we find ourselves somewhat reluctant to accept several chapters of the novel, particularly Chapters 26, 30 and 34, that contain almost interminable and tiring ruminations. Moreover, at times we do have a feeling that what this novel offers us is more of a Robert Jordan-Maria love story than anything else. And lastly, at least in patches, this novel strikes us as a routine sentimental exercise. The conversation that goes on between the wounded Robert Jordan, being left alone among the pine trees, and the anxiety-ridden Maria, gives us a taste of sentimental effusion:

> 'Listen to this well, rabbit,' he said. He knew there was a great hurry and he was sweating very much, but this had to be said and understood. 'Thou wilt go now, rabbit. But I go with thee. As long as there is one of us there is both of us. Do you understand?'
>
> 'Nay, I stay with thee.'

> 'Nay, rabbit. What I do now I do alone. I could not do it well with thee. If thou goest then I go, too. Do you not see how it is? Whichever one there is, is both.'[166]

We wonder if Robert Jordan, or for that matter, Hemingway, has the erudition, the mental training, the intellectual grit of a John Donne to save him from idle sentimentality.

Nevertheless, *For Whom the Bell Tolls* is a highly symbolical novel, and it is really worth the game to explore it as such.

The title of this novel takes us to one of John Donne's meditations, part of which is available to us as its epigraph. Though the stress in the novel's epigraph is on the theme of human solidarity, somehow or other Hemingway has not been able to drive this point home to us, with the result that he seems to be promoting the cause or cult of alienated individualism. The controversy about the novel in this regard is quite understandable.

However, the first important and outstanding symbol in *For Whom the Bell Tolls* comes to us in the form of the bridge that Robert Jordan has to blow up for the Republicans. It is worth noting that the word 'bridge' occurs for 294 times in the novel, and that while this word occurs for 32 times in Chapter I of the novel, it is used for 110 times in the last chapter of this book. As a symbol, the bridge stands for freedom, for hope for the future of human race itself. The second important symbol in the present novel is Maria's hair. Maria, as her very name implies, may be associated with the Virgin, but she is a 'violated virgin,'[167] for the Fascists have tortured and raped her and have got her head shaved mercilessly time and again. The loss of her hair suggests the loss of normal womanhood, while its gradual growth implies Maria's gradual return to balance and health.

As we have said earlier, the contrast between Republicanism and Fascism, between freedom and dictatorship, between man and machine, between the primitive society and the technological civilization, between Nature and the bombers that Hemingway offers in *For Whom the Bell Tolls* does have it own symbolic implications. And it is in this very light that we do also have to interpret the sport of bull-fight to which references are made in the novel, for besides being a typical Spanish sport, the bull-fight represents man's heroism, his masculine prowess, his capacity for endurance. The wheel symbol in the present novel suggests neither a wheel for a joy-ride nor the conventionally-accepted wheel of fortune; instead, as we have already pointed out, it suggests the wheel of human conflict.

The other two symbols that compel our attention in *For Whom the Bell Tolls* are Velazquez 63 and Gaylordś. Velazquez 63 is the headquarters of International Brigade, and it symbolizes the puritanical, austere and ritualistic kind of Communism that is taught and practised there. On the other hand, the Madrid hotel, Gaylordś, represents a kind of Communism that is based on conceit, deceitfulness and betrayal.

It is important to remember that the Fascist planes fly either in threes or in the formations of three, and that three is supposed to be a magical or mystical number. Similarly, the frequent use of the term *nada*, meaning *nothing* or *nothingness*, in the present novel suggests something sinister that is going to invade, disturb and destroy Spain's primitive culture and earthiness. And, as we have noted earlier rather in detail, the odour image that we come across in *For Whom the Bell Tolls* does have its own profound meaningfulness. In fact, almost all the images that Hemingway draws either from Nature or from the field of science do have their own appropriateness and appeal.

At the same time, it is also equally important to remember that almost all the major characters we encounter in the present novel are, in one way or another, closely connected with the bridge. The Chief of the demolition squad, Robert Jordan who is also the hero of the novel, is the very symbol of human freedom and dignity; Anselmo stands for a strict commitment to duty in spite of his severe hatred for violence; Rafael represents irresponsible paganism; Pablo is a veritable Judas, a symbol of the canker of defeatism, one who is afraid to die; Pilar, in spite of all her faults, is an archetypal Mother, the very image of primitivism, compassion and courage, while Maria symbolizes a longing for home.

In his essay entitled 'Hemingway's Ambiguity: Symbolism and Irony,' E.M. Halliday observes that 'the sleeping bag in *For Whom the Bell Tolls* is an obvious symbol of the womb.'[168] It is difficult to say anything else about Robert Jordan's sleeping bag, for it is inside this sleeping bag that the American dynamites and Maria make love.

For Whom the Bell Tolls contains a large number of symbols and images, and we can understand and appreciate the novel to the desired extent only if and when we comprehend the implications of these symbols and images.

REFERENCES

1. See Allen Guttmann, "Mechanized Doom:" Ernest Hemingway and the American View of the Spanish Civil War' in C. Baker (ed.), *Ernest Hemingway: Critiques of Four Major Novels* (New York , 1962), 95-107.
2. C. Baker, *Hemingway: The Writer as Artist* (Princeton, 1956), 251.
3. Baker 251.
4. Baker 251.
5. Baker 251.
6. Baker 250.
7. Baker 248.
8. Allen Guttmann, "Mechanized Doom:" Ernest Hemingway and the American View of the Spanish Civil War' in C. Baker (ed.) *Ernest Hemingway: Critiques of Four Major Novels* (New York, 1962), 98.
9. L. Trilling, 'An American in Spain,' *The Partisan Reader,* (eds.) W. Philips and P. Rahv (New York, 1946), 639.
10. Trilling 639.
11. Trilling 640.
12. Trilling 640.
13. Trilling 639.
14. Trilling 642.
15. A.C. Bessie, 'Review of *For Whom the Bell Tolls*,' *New Masses,* XXXVII (November 5, 1940), 25.
16. Bessie 25.

17. Bessie 25.
18. Bessie 26.
19. Bessie 29.
20. See Epigraph to *For Whom the Bell Tolls.*
21. C. Baker (ed.), *Ernest Hemingway: Critiques of Four Major Novels* (New York, 1962), 97.
22. A.C. Bessie, 'Review of *For Whom the Bell Tolls,' New Masses,* XXXVII (November 5, 1940), 28-29.
23. L. Trilling, 'An American in Spain,' *The Partisan Reader,* (eds.) W. Philips and P. Rahv (New York, 1946), 644.
24. M. Schorer, 'The Background of a Style,' *Kenyon Review,* iii (Winter, 1941), 103.
25. Ernest Hemingway, *For Whom the Bell Tolls* (Penguin edition, 1964), 45.
26. Hemingway 54.
27. Hemingway 37.
28. C. Baker (ed.) *Ernest Hemingway: Critiques of Four Major Novels* (New York, 1962), 98.
29. Ernest Hemingway, *For Whom the Bell Tolls* (Penguin edition, 1964), 65.
30. Hemingway 82.
31. Hemingway 19-20.
32. Hemingway 11.
33. Hemingway 19.
34. Hemingway 63.
35. Hemingway 132.
36. Hemingway 152.
37. Hemingway 158.
38. Hemingway 440.
39. C. Baker, *Hemingway: The Writer as Artist* (Princeton, 1956), 259.
40. Baker 259.
41. Baker 244.
42. Baker 244.
43. Ernest Hemingway, *For Whom the Bell Tolls,* (Penguin edition, 1964), 5.
44. Hemingway 42.
45. Hemingway 43.

46. Hemingway 44.
47. Hemingway 310-11.
48. Hemingway 273.
49. C. Baker, *Hemingway: The Writer as Artist* (Princeton, 1956), 243.
50. J.W. Beach, *American Fiction: 1920-1940* (New York, 1941), 116.
51. Beach 113.
52. Ernest Hemingway, *For Whom the Bell Tolls* (Penguin edition, 1964), 93.
53. Hemingway 21-22.
54. Hemingway 67.
55. Hemingway 263.
56. C. Baker, *Hemingway: The Writer as Artist* (Princeton, 1956), 244.
57. Baker, 252.
58. Ernest Hemingway, *For Whom the Bell Tolls* (Penguin edition, 1964), 13.
59. Hemingway 16.
60. Hemingway 16.
61. Hemingway 18.
62. Hemingway 53.
63. Hemingway 88.
64. Hemingway 270.
65. Hemingway 92.
66. C. Baker (ed.) *Ernest Hemingway: Critiques of Four Major Novels* (New York, 1962), 97.
67. Baker 251.
68. Baker 251.
69. Ernest Hemingway, *For Whom the Bell Tolls* (Penguin edition, 1964), 28.
70. Hemingway 294.
71. Hemingway 28.
72. Hemingway 89.
73. Hemingway 30.
74. Hemingway Chapter 10.
75. J.W. Beach, *American Fiction: 1920-1940* (New York, 1941), 113.
76. C. Baker (ed.) *Ernest Hemingway: Critiques of Four Major Novels* (New York, 1962), 98.

77. Baker 241.
78. Ernest Hemingway, *For Whom the Bell Tolls* (Penguin edition, 1964), 127.
79. C. Baker, *Hemingway: The Writer as Artist* (Princeton, 1956), 255-56.
80. M. Schorer, 'The Background of a Style', *Kenyon Review,* III (Winter, 1941), 104.
81. C. Baker, *Hemingway: The Writer as Artist* (Princeton, 1956), 256.
82. Baker 256.
83. Ernest Hemingway, *For Whom the Bell Tolls* (Penguin edition, 1964), 265.
84. Hemingway 418-19.
85. C. Baker, *Hemingway: The Writer as Artist* (Princeton, 1956), 244.
86. Baker 247.
87. See Ernest Hemingway, *For Whom the Bell Tolls* (Penguin edition, 1964), 5, 441.
88. Ernest Hemingway, *For Whom the Bell Tolls* (Penguin edition, 1964), 40.
89. Hemingway 85.
90. C. Baker, *Hemingway: The Writer as Artist* (Princeton, 1956), 258.
91. C. Baker (ed.) Ernest Hemingway: Critiques of Four Major Novels (New York, 1962), 95.
92. C. Baker 95.
93. Ernest Hemingway, *For Whom the Bell Tolls* (Penguin edition, 1964), 284.
94. Hemingway 73-74.
95. Hemingway 304.
96. C. Baker, *Hemingway: The Writer as Artist* (Princeton, 1956), 253.
97. See Ernest Hemingway, *For Whom the Bell Tolls* (Penguin edition, 1964), 263.
98. Hemingway 282.
99. Hemingway 22.
100. Hemingway 22.
101. Hemingway 22.
102. Hemingway 438.
103. Hemingway 404.
104. Hemingway 407.

105. See Hemingway 101, 110, 126, 136, 137, 176, 177, 178, 184, 230, 232, & 344.
106. See Ernest Hemingway, *For Whom the Bell Tolls* (Penguin edition, 1964), 130.
107. C. Baker, *Hemingway: The Writer as Artist* (Princeton, 1956), 260.
108. C. Baker (ed.) *Ernest Hemingway: Critiques of Four Major Novels* (New York, 1962), 96.
109. Hemingway 216.
110. See Ernest Hemingway, *For Whom the Bell Tolls* (Penguin edition, 1964), 216.
111. Hemingway 217.
112. C. Baker, *Hemingway: The Writer as Artist* (Princeton, 1956), 262.
113. Baker 262.
114. Baker 263.
115. Baker 263.
116. Ernest Hemingway, For Whom the Bell Tolls (Penguin edition, 1964), 225-26.
117. Hemingway 225.
118. Hemingway 225.
119. Hemingway 225.
120. Hemingway 220.
121. Hemingway 221.
122. Hemingway 222.
123. Hemingway 221.
124. Hemingway 59.
125. Hemingway 94.
126. Hemingway119.
127. Hemingway 123.
128. Hemingway 155.
129. Hemingway 216.
130. Hemingway 241.
131. Hemingway 275.
132. Hemingway 318.
133. Hemingway 378.
134. Hemingway 246.
135. Hemingway 249.

136. Hemingway 21.
137. Hemingway 151.
138. Hemingway 68.
139. Hemingway 28.
140. Hemingway 28.
141. Hemingway 25.
142. Hemingway 30.
143. Hemingway 28.
144. Hemingway 205.
145. Hemingway 206.
146. Hemingway 207.
147. Hemingway 132.
148. Hemingway 167.
149. Hemingway 168.
150. Hemingway 132.
151. Hemingway 145.
152. Hemingway 312.
153. Hemingway 371.
154. Hemingway 375.
155. Hemingway 409.
156. Hemingway 179.
157. Hemingway 309.
158. Hemingway 32.
159. Hemingway 49.
160. Hemingway 75.
161. Hemingway 75.
162. Hemingway 85.
163. C. Baker, Hemingway: *The Writer as Artist* (Princeton, 1956), 248.
164. Baker 248.
165. Baker 248.
166. Ernest Hemingway, *For Whom the Bell Tolls* (Penguin edition, 1964), 436.
167. See Melvin Backman, 'Hemingway: The Matador and the Crucified,' *Modern Fiction Studies*, 1 (August 1955), 7.
168. E.M. Halliday, 'Hemingway's Ambiguity: Symbolism and Irony,' *American Literature* XXVIII, (March, 1956), 4.

5

The Old Man and the Sea

'CRITICS HAVE become,' says Joseph Waldmeir, 'increasingly suspicious that it is necessary to read Hemingway's work on the symbolic as well as on the story level in order to gain a full appreciation of its art. Since the publication of *The Old Man and the Sea,* the suspicion has become first an awareness, then a certainty.'[1] *The Old Man and the Sea* came out in 1952; in 1953 it earned Hemingway the Pulitzer Prize in Fiction, and it was only next year, that is, in 1954, that Hemingway received the award of the Nobel Prize for literature. *The Old Man and the Sea* is a short novel of nearly one hundred and twenty-five pages, and it may, as such, be regarded as a novelette, or else as a long short story. And, after we have gone through it, we do realize that its story is as interesting and exciting as its symbolism is profound and meaningful. The story of this book deals neither with victory nor with defeat; it may be said to deal with both victory and defeat, but in any case it does recount Santiago's epic struggle against the forces of nature. In fact, it is in this struggle itself, and not in victory or defeat, that the enduring significance of this book lies.

Relying on Hemingway's statement that the 'dignity of movement of an iceberg is due to only one-eighth of it being above water,'[2] Clinton S. Burhans Jr. maintains that with all its Christian symbolism, *The Old Man and the Sea* is a study in 'the relationship between individualism and interdependence,'[3] in 'the agony of active and isolated individualism in a universe which dooms such individualism.'[4] In his comments on Hemingway's fictional works, Carlos Baker observes that what we find in them is a peculiar amalgam of realism and symbolism. He says:

> Goethe called his autobiography *Dichtung and Wahrheit,* Poetry and Truth. The reverse of Goethe's title, as a strategy of emphasis, admirably fits the collected works of Hemingway. From the first he has been dedicated as a writer to the rendering of *Wahrheit,* the precise and at least partly naturalistic presentation of things as they are and were. Yet under all his brilliant surfaces lies the controlling *Dichtung,* the symbolic underpainting which gives so remarkable a sense of depth and vitality to what might otherwise seem flat and two-demensional.[5]

And, speaking pointedly about *The Old Man and the Sea,* he goes on to say: 'This short novel, in the words of Eliot, explores yet "another intensity" beyond those which can be located in Hemingway's previous fictions. Among the vast waters of the petrel and the porpoise, he seemed to many of his readers to have found the means of establishing "a further union" and "a deeper communion" between *Wahrheit* and *Dichtung* than he had achieved before.'[6] In his paper on *The Old Man and the Sea,* Joseph Waldmeir, while acknowledging the use of religious symbols in this novel, lays stress on the point that what Hemingway is really committed to is not orthodox religion, but the Religion of Man. He states:

> Hemingway did not turn religious to write *The Old Man and the Sea.* He has always been religious, though his religion is not of the orthodox, organized variety. He celebrates, he has always celebrated, the Religion of Man: *The Old Man and the Sea* merely celebrates it more forcefully and convincingly than any previous Hemingway work. It is the final step in the celebration.[7]

In his turn, Melvin Backman comes out with the view that the two motifs which run right from *In Our Time* to *The Old Man and the Sea* are those of 'the matador and the crucified,'[8] of the sacrificer and the sacrificed. He further says:

> When we reach *The Old Man and the Sea,* we seem to have come a long way from the early works, but there is

> a pattern into which all of them fall. It is true that the old man is the only hero who is not left alone, at the end of the story, with death or despair. He is old and womanless and humble. Yet in him we have a blending of the two dominant motifs—the matador and the crucified.[9]

And Mark Schorer maintains that Hemingway's art, 'when it is art, is absolutely incomparable,'[10] that Hemingway is unquestionably the greatest craftsman in the American novel in this century,[11] that *The Old Man and the Sea* 'appears to be not only a moral fable, but a parable,'[12] and that 'all the taut excitment in the prose comes...from the parable.'[13]

The title of *The Old Man and the Sea* is too simple and clear to call for any explanation; this novel tells us about the adventure and struggle of an old man, an old fisherman named Santiago, who, after months of failure and disappointment, goes far out on the sea, catches a huge fish all by himself on the eighty-fifth day, struggles with the fish in a spirit of love and hate, and resists the sharks with all the fierceness and strength at his command, but who, after all this ordeal, is able to bring to the shore only the skeleton of the huge fish.

It is thus that we come to a detailed study of the symbols in the present novel.

II

As we go through *The Old Man and the Sea,* we find that it is the old fisherman, Santiago, who is projected as the main symbol in the novel, and that all other symbols, including the sea as a symbol, revolve round this very main symbol. Santiago, says the novelist, 'was an old man who fished alone in a skiff in the Gulf Stream and he had gone eighty-four days now without taking a fish.'[14] For the first forty days a boy named Manolin accompanies him on his fishing expedition, but since nothing comes out of these fishing trips, it is on the persuasion of his parents that the boy has to stop going out with him. Santiago is considered to be 'definitely and finally *salao,* which is the worst form of unlucky.'[15] And yet, he does not lose heart; his 'hope and his confidence,' as the author puts it, 'had never gone.'[16] Hemingway speaks of his eyes that are 'cheerful and undefeated,'[17] of his 'sun-burned, confident loving eyes,'[18] and of his 'faith'[19] in himself. He has the grains of both humility and pride in his character; he 'had attained humility...he knew he had attained it and he knew it was not disgraceful and it carried no loss of true pride.'[20] Santiago calls himself 'a strange old man'[21] and thinks that he is 'strong enough now for a truly big fish.'[22] Moreover, the old fisherman says: 'I may not be as strong as I think.... But I know many tricks and I have resolution.'[23] Santiago is indeed a man of tremendous determination.

It is on the eighty-fifth day that Santiago is enthused by a new kind of confidence. 'Every day,' he thinks, 'is a new day;'[24] he goes on to think of better and still better days ahead, so that 'when luck comes you are ready.'[25] He watches 'the flying fish burst out again and again and the ineffectual movements of the bird;'[26] he looks, almost dreamily, at them, and in view of all these movements he fondly hopes that his 'big fish must be somewhere'[27] around. It is indeed Santiago's great, good luck that on this day he hooks a giant fish, of the size of which he has absolutely no idea, at least on the first day and the following night. 'One hundred fathoms down,' he could realize, 'a marlin was eating the sardines that covered the point and the shank of the hook where the hand-forged hook projected from the head of the small tuna.'[28] He holds the line delicately with his left hand, unleashes it from the stick, and lets it run through his fingers without the fish feeling any tension. And it is thus that his struggle with the 'huge'[29] fish begins, which goes on and on for two days and two nights until such time as it is killed and the sharks arrive to eat its flesh.

It is only on the second day that Santiago gets just a fleeting view of the fish. 'The line rose slowly and steadily and then the surface of the ocean bulged ahead of the boat and the fish came out.'[30] And as it re-enters the water, the line goes out fast along with it, and it does not at all seem to have 'panicked.'[31] But even before Santiago has seen the fish, his experience tells him that it is really a huge, gigantic fish. 'He was happy,' says the novelist, feeling the gentle pulling and then he felt something hard and unbelievably heavy. It was the weight of the fish and he let the line slip down, down, down, unrolling off the first of the two reserve coils.[32] And the novelist goes on to say that as the line 'went down, slipping lightly through the old man's fingers, he still could feel the great weight....'[33] Naturally enough, such terms as 'what a fish,'[34] 'a huge fish,'[35] 'a great fish'[36] and 'a strong full-blooded fish'[37] are used for Santiago's catch, though he does not want the fish to be conscious of its strength. 'I must never,' thinks the old fisherman, 'let him learn his strength nor what he could do if he made his run. If I were him I would put in everything now and go until something broke. But, thank God, they are not as intelligent as we who kill them; although they are more noble and more able.'[38] When Santiago gets a clear and full view of the fish for the first time, he finds it difficult to believe his eyes:

> It was on the third turn that he saw the fish first. He saw him first as a dark shadow that took so long to pass under the boat that he could not believe its length. 'No,' he said. 'He can't be that big.'[39]

And as people look at the skeleton of this fish, which alone Santiago has been able to carry to the shore after all his ordeals and pains, they express their feeling of hushed amazement at the sight of 'a great long white spine with a huge tail at the end that lifted and swung with the tide.'[40] Santiago, as Hemingway puts it, 'was fast to the biggest fish that he had ever seen and bigger than he had ever heard of.'[41]

It is with this kind of formidable fish that the old fisherman has to grapple. Placed precariously in his boat, but trying to make himself as comfortable there as he could do so, he moves about with the fish far out on the sea for two days and two nights, and it is only late in the afternoon on the third day that he is able to kill it. His case is one of intense struggle, of great suffering and of terrific endurance. Santiago 'settled comfortably against the wood and took his suffering as it came and the fish swam steadily and the boat moved slowly through the dark water.'[42] He, as the novelist says once again, 'was comfortable but suffering, although he did not admit the suffering at all.'[43] It is by necessity and 'choice'[44] that he has to stay on in the deep dark water of the sea all alone, 'far out beyond all snares and traps and treacheries.'[45] And it is not just the fact that Santiago is the pursuer or the hunter, he is also very much the pursued or the hunted, and he has to suffer, to undergo pains in both the capacities. Nevertheless, as he says, 'pain does not matter to a man.'[46] He is determined and tenacious enough to assure himself that he would show the fish 'what a man can do and what a man endures,'[47] and he comes out with his motto when he says that 'man is not made for defeat,'[48] or that a man 'can be destroyed but not defeated.'[49] Santiago is the very image, the very symbol of endurance, determination, tenacity and resolution.

However, this is but one aspect of Santiago's character. Santiago, as we have already said, does not have only humility and pride and confidence in himself, he does also have love and affection for birds and turtles and other creatures of the sea. He, says the novelist, 'was very fond of flying fish as they were his principal friends on the ocean. He was sorry for the birds, especially the small delicate dark terns that were always flying and looking and almost never finding.'[50] And the old fisherman says: 'The bird is a great help.'[51] At the same, time it is also equally profitable to take due note of Santiago's reaction to the presence of a male and a female porpoise near his boat:

> During the night two porpoise came around the boat and he could hear them rolling and blowing. He could tell the difference between the blowing noise the male made and the sighing blow of the female.
>
> 'They are good,' he said.
>
> 'They play and make jokes and love one another. They are our brothers like the flying fish.'[52]

Santiago loves 'green turtles and hawks-bills with their elegance and speed and their great value.'[53] The novelist goes on to say:

> He had no mysticism about turtles although he had gone in turtle boats for many years. He was so sorry for them all, even the great trunkbacks that were as long as the skiff and weighed a ton. Most people are heartless about turtles because a turtle's heart will beat for hours after he has been cut up and butchered. But the old man thought, I have such a heart too and my feet and hands are like theirs.[54]

It is this very kind of attitude, an attitude based on love and affection and sympathy, that Santiago holds out to the big fish.

This big fish is his enemy, his foe, his adversary, and yet it is his friend. He wants the marlin to eat more and more of the bait so that the hook goes into its heart and kills it. And even as he says that he would stay with it until he is dead,[55] he does know that he and the fish 'are joined together.'[56] He begins to 'pity'[57] the fish, for it is 'wonderful and strange and who knows how old.'[58] This friend-foe relationship becomes clear when Santiago says: 'Fish...I love you and respect you. But I will kill you before this day ends.'[59] The old fisherman is a desperate character; he has to catch the fish either dead or alive, but he wonders if the fish too has 'any plans,'[60] or if it is just as 'desperate'[61] as he himself is. In any case, the epic fight between the two continues. 'The fish is my friend too,' Santiago speaks to himself. 'I have never seen or heard of such a fish. But I must kill him.'[62] Santiago, says the novelist, 'was sorry for the great fish that had nothing to eat and his determination to kill him never relaxed in his sorrow for him.'[63] However, he is so very respectful towards the fish when he thinks that there is no one worthy of eating him from the manner of his behaviour and his great dignity.[64] Nevertheless, the old fisherman says: 'Fish, you are going to have to die anyway. Do you have to kill me too?'[65] And it is in such a frame of mind that he thinks: 'You are killing me, fish.... But you have a right to. Never have I seen a greater, or more beautiful, or a calmer or more noble thing than you, brother. Come on and kill me. I do not care who kills who.'[66] But since enough is enough, Santiago, as the novelist puts it, 'took all his pain and what was left of his strength and his long gone pride and he put it against the fish's agony and the fish came over to his side and swam gently on his side, his bill almost touching the planking of the skiff, and started to pass the boat, long, deep, wide, silver and barred with purple and intermindable in the water.'[67] It is indeed very graphically and poignantly that Hemingway describes the manner in which Santiago kills the fish:

> The old man dropped the line and put his foot on it and lifted the harpoon as high as he could and drove it down with all his strength, and more strength he had just summoned, into the fish's side just behind the great chest fin that rose high in the air to the altitude of the man's chest. He felt the iron go in and he leaned on it and drove it further and then pushed all his weight after it.[68]

The huge fish, weighing over fifteen hundred pounds, is dead. It is not at all unnatural for the tired old Santiago to say mournfully: 'I have killed the fish which is my brother, and now I must do the slave work.'[69]

At this point it is important to note that this big fish or marlin, Santiago's prize catch, is one of the major symbols in *The Old Man and the Sea*. Santiago first wonders whether it is a dram or reality; subsequently, he does feel 'the strength of the great fish:' [70] a specific mention is made of its 'great length and width,'[71] of all its 'power and...beauty,'[72] and Hemingway, very strikingly and powerfully, presents to us the terrific beauty of this great fish:

> His sword was a long as a baseball bat and tapered like a rapier and he rose his full length from the water and then re-entered it, smoothly, like a diver and the old man saw the great scythe-blade of his tail go under....[73]

This huge fish is a marvel of creation; it is mystery, a miracle of Nature's inventiveness, and it may be said to be a complete achievement in itself. 'The great marlin,' says Clinton S. Burhans Jr., 'is unlike the other fish which the old man catches; he is a spiritual more than a physical necessity.'[74] And in his essay on *The Old Man and the Sea,* Carlos Baker comments that 'within the structure of the story, it may be said at once, the gallantry of Santiago is defined in part by the gallantry of his adversary.'[75] And when the sharks mutilate the fish, Santiago does not feel like looking at it. 'He did not like to look at the fish any more since he had been mutilated. When the fish had been hit it was as though he himself were hit.'[76]

It hardly requires explaining that the blood of the gallant but dead fish attracts the sharks and the first shark hits the fish within an hour of its death:

> The shark was not an accident. He had come up from deep down in the water as the dark cloud of blood had settled and dispersed in the mile-deep sea. He had come up so fast and absolutely without caution that he broke the surface of the blue water and was in the sun. Then he fell back into the sea and picked up the scent and started swimming on the course the skiff and the fish had taken.[77]

The sharks come in ones, twos, threes, and then in clusters, and devour the carcass of the fish doggedly and mercilessly. Santiago fights out the sharks as resolutely and desperately as he can do so, but he finds it increasingly difficult, if not impossible, to protect the fish against their attack. 'They were,' says the novelist, 'hateful sharks, bad-smelling, scavengers as well as killers, and when they were hungry they would bite at an oar or the rudder of a boat.'[78] Santiago even tries to rationalize this disaster by thinking that 'everything kills everything else in some way;'[79] all the same, by the time he reaches the Havana shore after nearly seventy-two hours, the fish has been reduced to a huge, mind-boggling skeleton. And as he climbs up the coast and looks back at the fish, what he finds there is shockingly true. Santiago 'stopped for a moment and looked back and saw in the reflection from the street light the great tail of the fish standing up well behind the skiff's tern. He saw the white naked line of his backbone and the dark mass of the head with the projecting bill and all the nakedness between.'[80] In *The Old Man and the Sea,* the sharks too constitute an important and powerful symbol. And in this connection, in his essay entitled 'Hemingway: The Matador and the Crucified,' Melvin Backman observes:

> The old man beating off the sharks is like life rebelling against death—as though the old man and the great fish who are lashed together and steering as one toward home, just as earlier they had been bound by the 'pain of life,' have become the symbol of life; while the sharks (scavengers like the vultures and hyena who are symbols of death in 'The Snows of Kilimanjaro') have become the death which must be resisted even though it will win.[81]

It is not at all difficult to see that if Santiago and the big fish stand for life, then the sharks—the killers and the scavengers—symbolize death.

It is true that Santiago has moved far out on the sea, and it is quite consciously that Hemingway employs the term 'far out' several times in the present novel. And even as Santiago says that he would fight against the sharks until he is dead,[82] he does also realize that he should not have gone out so far on the sea. He tells himself: 'I shouldn't have gone out so far, fish.... Neither for you nor for me. I'm sorry, fish.'[83] As we find it, the 'sea' is a major factor and indeed a major symbol in *The Old Man and the Sea*. The sea is 'kind and very beautiful,'[84] but it can also be 'so cruel.'[85] Hemingway describes so very clearly what the old fisherman and the other fishermen think of the sea:

> He always thought of the sea as *la mar* which is what people call her in Spanish when they love her. Sometimes those who love her say bad things of her but they are always said as though she were a woman. Some of the younger fishermen, those who used buoys as floats for their lines and had motor-boats, bought when the shark livers had brought much money, spoke of her as *el mar* which is masculine. They spoke of her as a contestant or a place or even an enemy. But the old man always thought of her as feminine and as something that gave or withheld great favours, and if she did wild or wicked things it was because she could not help them. The moon affects her as it does a woman, he thought.[86]

And it is not without reason that Hemingway describes Santiago as looking at the sky above and into 'the dark of the water'[87] below, and thinking so often of his loneliness in the vast space around. 'He looked across the sea,' says Hemingway, 'and knew how alone he was now.'[88] The sea has its own mystery, its own strangeness; it has its own immensity, and it may be said to symbolize the splendour of cosmic vastness. In a way, Santiago has violated the sanctity, the privacy of the forbidden zone; he has committed transgression, and seen in this light he has perpetrated an evil, a sin. And much though he thinks about the sin of transgression and the sin of despair, he tells himself: 'Do not think about sin.... There are enough problems now without sin. Also I have no understanding of it.'[89] And still he goes on to think about sin:

> I have no understanding of it and I am not sure that I believe in it. Perhaps it was a sin to kill the fish. I suppose it was even though I did it to keep me alive and feed many people. But then everything is a sin. Do not think about sin. It is much too late for that and there are people who are paid to do it. Let them think about it. You were born to be a fisherman as the fish was born to be a fish.[90]

'I am not religious,'[91] says Santiago, and yet he thinks about both pride and sin:

> ...he liked to think about all things that he was involved in and since there was nothing to read and he did not have a radio, he thought much and he kept on thinking about sin. You did not kill the fish only to keep alive and to sell for food, he thought. You killed him for pride and because you are a fisherman. You loved him when he was alive and you loved him after. If you love him, it is not a sin to kill him. Or is it more?[92]

Commenting upon this problem of evil or sin, Clinton S. Burhans Jr. observes that 'in killing the great marlin and in losing him to the sharks, that old man learns the sin into which men inevitably fall by going far out beyond their depth, beyond true place in life,'[93] that 'when the sharks came, it is almost as a thing expected, almost as a punishment which the old man brings upon himself in going far out...and there hooking and killing the great flsh,'[94] and that 'the old man senses an inevitability in the coming of the sharks, a feeling of guild which deepens into remorse and regret.'[95]

Understandably enough, it is the religious or Christian symbolism in *The Old Man and the Sea* that is of profound interest to us. Santiago does not seem to have to do anything with Christianity; nevertheless, he leaves his wife's relics undisturbed. 'On the brown walls of the flattened, overlapping leaves of the sturdy fibred *guano* there was a picture in colour of the Sacred Heart of Jesus and another of the Virgin of Cobre. These were relics of his wife.'[96] At the same time, it is also equally important to take note of the fact that he thinks of and speaks out in the name of Christ when the big fish is about to be hooked and when he gets a vague idea of the huge size of marlin. 'Christ knows,' says Santiago, 'he can't have gone;'[97] or, 'Christ,' says he, 'I didn't know he was so big.'[98] Moreover, it is indeed significant that we see the old fisherman offering prayers so that he may be able to catch the big fish:

> '...I will say ten Our Fathers and ten Hail Marys that I should catch this fish, and I promise to make a pilgrimage to the Virgin de Cobre if I catch him.... Hail Mary full of Grace the Lord is with thee. Blessed art thou among women and blessed is the fruit of thy womb, Jesus. Holy Mary, Mother of God, pray for us sinners now and at the hour of our death. Amen. Blessed Virgin, pray for the death of this fish....'[99]

Santiago undergoes every possible pain and suffering to be able to catch the fish or to kill it, and this element of pain or suffering coupled with the twin elements of piety and compassion for the fish, does have its own Christian association. And in the present novel we get the first inkling of Crucifixion in Santiago's uninhibited, spontaneous reaction to the arrival of sharks near the dead fish:

> 'Ayo,' he said aloud. There is no translation for this word and perhaps it is just a noise such as a man might make, involuntarily, feeling the nail go through his hands and into the wood.[100]

As the old fisherman reaches the shore with the skeleton of the huge fish, there is none to receive and help him there. 'He unstepped the mast and furled the sail and tied it. Then he shouldered the mast and started to climb. It was then that he knew the depth of his tiredness.'[101] Like Jesus going up the Calvary hills, he too starts climbing the hilly coast. 'He started to climb...and at the top he fell and lay for some time with the mast across his shoulder. He tried to get up. But it was too difficult and he sat there with the mast on his shoulder and looked at the road. A cat passed on the far side going about its business and the old man watched it.'[102] Finally, he 'put the mast down and stood up. He picked the mast up and put it on his shoulder and started up the road. He had to sit down five times before he reached his shack.'[103] And as Hemingway gives us Santiago's picture in sleep 'with his arms out straight and the palm of his hands up,'[104] we immediately see his resemblance with Christ, and the very phenomenon of Crucifixion is brought vividly before us.

In his essay on *The Old Man and the Sea,* Carlos Baker says:

> In its main outlines, the story is simple. Stripped, like the marlin, down to its bare bones, it looks not unlike the 200-word version which Hemingway first recorded in an article on the Gulf Stream during the spring of 1936.... The difference between this anecdote and the finished work of art is immense[105] (See Appendix A).

And he states further that in 'a strictly objective view, the man Santiago is only a simple fisherman, like his namesake the son of Zebedee, mending his nets by the shore of Galiee[106] and that Santiago 'shows, in his own right, certain qualities of mind and heart which are clearly associated with the character and personality of Jesus Christ in the Gospel stories.'[107] According to Mark Schorer, the old man has 'a Franciscan quality that so pervades his habit of thought as to support and give the body of dramatic plausibility, even inevitability to the suggestion of Christian martyrdom which comes at the end.'[108] In his turn, Joseph Waldmeir speaks of the 'Christian religious symbols running through it,'[109] and observes:

> The Christian symbolism so evident here shifts from man to fish—a legitimate symbol for Christ since the beginning of Christianity, as it was a legitimate religious symbol before Christianity— and back to man throughout the story.[110]

Referring to the Christian numerology, Waldmeir says that 'three, seven, and forty are key numbers in the Old and New Testaments, and in the religion, and that Hemingway makes a judicious use of them.'[111] In his essay captioned 'Hemingway: The Matador and the Crucified,' Melvin Backman states that Santiago is 'Spanish for Saint James—the fisherman, apostle, and martyr from the Sea of Galilee'[112] and that 'suffering and gentle and wood blend magically into an image of Christ on the cross.'[113]

Besides these major symbols—Santiago, marlin, the sea and the sharks—in *The Old Man and the Sea*, there are other symbols as well in it in the form of the boy, Manolin, Santiago's love for the baseball, and his dreams.

Manolin had been working with Santiago since he was five years old, and the 'old man had taught the boy to fish and the boy loved him.'[114] In his days of distress and misfortune too, the boy accompanies Santiago on the sea for forty days, and then he has to leave his company on the orders of his parents. Even so, as we find, he takes full care of the old fisherman and makes available to him all the provisions that he requires. In fact, the boy looks upon Santiago as 'the best fisherman,'[115] and declares: "*Que' va*....There are many good fishermen and some great ones. But there is only you.'[116] This acknowledgement makes it amply clear to us that there is a teacher-taught relationship between Santiago and Manolin, and that the old fisherman is almost the boy's adopted father. Moreover, it is for nine times that Santiago remembers boy while he is all alone far out on the sea. He murmurs to himself: 'I wish I had the boy;'[117] or 'I wish the boy were here;'[118] or, "I wish the boy were here."[119] It is not at all difficult to see that Santiago remembers the boy for his help and support chiefly because in him he sees the very image of his lost youth and manhood. Perhaps, that is why, earlier, he tells Manolin: 'You are already a man.'[120] Joseph Waldmeir does rightly comment that the old fisherman is 'also a teacher, one who taught the boy not only how to fish—that is, how to make a living—but how to behave as well, giving him the pride and humility necessary to a good life.'[121] And in this connection Carlos Baker says that we just cannot 'discount Manolin's dramatic function, which is to heighten our sympathy for the old fisherman,'[122] that 'Manolin's love for Santiago is that of a disciple for a master in the arts of fishing,'[123] that 'it is also the love of a son for an adopted father,'[124] and that through agency of Manolin Santiago is 'able to recapture in his imagination, and therefore to a certain degree in fact, the same strength and confidence which distinguished his own young manhood as a fisherman and earned him the title of *El Campeon*.'[125]

Once again, it is in a similar manner that we may consider Santiago's passion for the baseball game. No doubt, Santiago is a heroic individual, and still when he remembers the boy while he is all alone far out on the sea, besides recalling his own youth, he does also show his respect for human solidarity and interdependence. The game of baseball, of which DiMaggio is the champion, depends far more on team-work than the highly individualistic sport of bull-fighting or fishing. And when Santiago speaks of 'the great DiMaggio'[126] and says that DiMaggio 'does all things perfectly even with the pain of the bone spur in his heel,'[127] he looks upon him as a symbol of strength, determination and endurance, which Santiago himself is.

Thinking of 'many years ago,'[128] Santiago tells Manolin: 'When I was your age I was before the mast on a square-rigged ship that ran to Africa and I have seen lions on the beaches in the evening.'[129] And when he goes to sleep, he dreams of 'Africa when he was a boy and the long, golden beaches and the white beaches, so white they hurt your eyes, and the high capes and the great brown mountains.'[130] As the novelist puts it, he 'no longer dreamed of storms, nor of women, nor of great occurrences, nor of great fish, nor fights, nor contests of strength, nor of his wife.

He only dreamed of places now and of the lions on the beach. They played like young cats in the dusk and he loved them as he loved the boy.'[131] Even at the time when he is struggling with the fish, he wishes he 'could sleep and dream about the lions.'[132] It is not at all unnatural for him to ask himself: 'Why are the lions the main thing that is left?'[133] Later, when he does really fall asleep in his boat on the sea, he starts dreaming again:

> ...he began to dream of the long yellow beach and he saw the first of the lions came down onto it in the early dark and then the other lions came and he rested his chin on the wood of the bows where the ship lay anchored with the evening offshore breeze and he waited to see if there would be more lions.[134]

Expectedly enough, at the close of the novel where we find him again in sleep in his shack after a long stint of stress and strain, hardship and failure, we find him 'dreaming about the lions.'[135] Lions are an obsession, a fixation with him, first because they are a source of his wish-fulfilment, a compensation for what he has not been able to achieve in life, and secondly because they are the highest models of strength and courage. This dream of lions is an evocative symbol; it is organically connected with the symbol of the boy, and when Carlos Baker speaks of 'the double vision of the boy and the lions,'[136] what he suggests is that 'the boy and the lions are related to one of the fundamental psychological laws of Santiago's—and indeed of human—nature: the constant wavelike operation of bracing and relaxation.'[137] Baker further says that the 'boy braces, the lions relax, as in the systolic-diastolic movement of the human heart.'[138]

III

Apart from the symbols we have considered at length, in *The Old Man and the Sea* we come across a number of images that have their own relevance and value. Perhaps, Santiago's feeling of despair on account of his failure for eighty-four days in a row could not have been expressed better than by stating that the 'sail was patched with flour sacks and, furled, it looked like the flag of permanent defeat.'[139] And Hemingway does succeed in describing graphically the scars on the old fisherman's hands when he says that 'none of these scars were fresh'[140] and that they 'were as old as erosions in a fishless desert.'[141] It is indeed interesting to find that the novelist compares the clubbing of a fish to the 'chopping of a tree.'[142] Hemingway, we see, draws most of his images from Nature. Speaking about the deep dark water of sea, he points to 'the strange undulation of the calm;'[143] describing the white clouds hanging over the sea, he presents to us a picture of 'the white cumulus built like friendly piles of ice-cream;'[144] he says that 'the fish's eye looked as detached as the mirrors in a periscope or as a saint in a procession,'[145] and describing the arrival of a shark near Santiago's boat, the novelist says: he 'came like a pig to the trough if a pig had a mouth so wide that you could put your head in it.'[146] As Santiago is struggling with the huge marlin on the second night, he finds himself enveloped in the darkness of the starless sky, and Hemingway describes the whole scene so very vividly when he says: 'The sky was clouding over to the east and one after another the stars he knew were gone. It looked now as though he were moving into a great canyon of clouds.'[147] Moreover, the novelist gives us a host of olfactory images when he speaks of 'the sweet blood smell'[148] of the fish, 'the smell of Africa,'[149] 'the smell of the land breeze,'[150] and of 'the clean early morning smell of the ocean.'[151]

Most of these images are highly sensuous and evocative, and they do create a kind of atmosphere that heightens the effect of Santiago's loneliness and his struggle with the big fish and the sharks.

IV

A close and careful study of *The Old Man and the Sea* gives us a definite impression of the fact that here is a novel, the scope of which is not just limited to a presentation of realistic details about an old fisherman's desperate and protracted struggle with a huge fish and the sharks; instead, we do realize that here is a novel which is indeed a successful work of art, poetic, symbolical, full of images, and ambiguous in a rich and positive sense. As we have seen earlier, Santiago is not merely the symbol of strength, endurance and determination, he does also stand for love and affection, pride and humility, piety and compassion. There are enough hints in the novel to suggest that Santiago is a Christ-like figure, that his suffering and nobility do constitute what we may call the phenomenon of Crucifixion, and that the novel does have its own Christian or religious association. Moreover, there are two qualities in his character, his heroic individualism and his patience, that remind us necessarily of Job. Similarly, the huge fish, Santiago's prize catch, is not only the marvel of creation, it is also something akin to Christ, for, as we have pointed out earlier, fish has been traditionally associated with Christ. The next symbol that deserves mention at this point comes to us in the form of the sharks which represent the forces of death and destruction. In its own turn, the sea, with all its depth and vastness, symbolizes both mystery and immensity, and Santiago's feeling of loneliness during his drift on the sea is quite natural and understandable.

As we have said earlier, the boy, Manolin, is Santiago's disciple, and the relationship between the boy and the old fisherman is that between the taught and his teacher, a son and his adopted father. However, the boy in the novel is a symbol of the old fisherman's remembrance of his youth, of his craving for immortality, and it is no wonder that from, to time during his days of loneliness and stress, Santiago wishes the boy to be with himself. Likewise, the old fisherman's occasional dreams relating to Africa and its lions are a symbolic pointer to his strength and tenacity during his youth. These dreams, we have said, serve the purpose of psychological stimulus to Santiago; they are a sort of wish-fulfilment, a kind of compensation for what he has not been able to achieve in life. Similarly, the baseball player, DiMaggio, is Santiago's favourite; the old fisherman speaks of him or remembers him at several places in the novel, and he uses the word 'great' almost repeatedly for him. These references to DiMaggio reflected not only Santiago's passion for the baseball game, they do also heighten his feeling for teamwork, for solidarity, for human interdependence at a time when he is all alone on the sea, facing the challenge of his grim encounter with the fish and the sharks.

It is important to remember that Santiago, a name that takes us to Saint James, a fisherman, apostle and martyr from the Sea of Galilee, is the central symbol in *The Old Man and the Sea* and that all the other symbols of this novel revolve round this very central symbol.

REFERENCES

1. J. Waldmeir, 'Confiteor Hominem: Ernest Hemingway's Religion of Man,' Papers of the Michigan Academy of Science, Arts and Letters, XLII (Michigan, 1957), 349.
2. Ernest Hemingway, *Death in the Afternoon* (New York, 1932), 183.
3. Clinton S. Burhans Jr., *'The Old Man and the Sea:* Hemingway's Tragic Vision of Man,' *American Literature,* xxxi (Jan., 1960), 447.
4. Burhans 447.
5. C. Baker, *Hemingway: The Writer as Artist* (Princeton, 1956), 289.
6. Baker 291.
7. J. Waldmeir, 'Confiteor Hominem: Ernest Hemingway's Religion of Man,' Papers of the Michigan Academy of Science, Arts, and Letters, XLII (Michigan, 1957), 356.
8. C. Baker (ed.) *Hemingway and His Critics: An International Anthology* (New York, 1961), 245.
9. Baker 257.
10. M. Schorer, 'With Grace under Pressure,' *New Republic,* CXXVII (Oct. 6, 1952), 20.
11. Schorer 20.
12. Schorer 20.
13. Schorer 20.
14. Ernest Hemingway, *The Old Man and the Sea* (Moscow, 1967), 33.
15. Hemingway 33.
16. Hemingway 36.
17. Hemingway 33.
18. Hemingway 36.
19. Hemingway 34.
20. Hemingway 36.

21. Hemingway 37.
22. Hemingway 37.
23. Hemingway 43.
24. Hemingway 50.
25. Hemingway 50.
26. Hemingway 51.
27. Hemingway 51.
28. Hemingway 56.
29. Hemingway 56.
30. Hemingway 71.
31. Hemingway 71.
32. Hemingway 57.
33. Hemingway 57.
34. Hemingway 57.
35. Hemingway 57.
36. Hemingway 61.
37. Hemingway 69.
38. Hemingway 71-72.
39. Hemingway 90-91.
40. Hemingway 116-17.
41. Hemingway 72.
42. Hemingway 72.
43. Hemingway 72.
44. Hemingway 62.
45. Hemingway 62.
46. Hemingway 87.
47. Hemingway 74.
48. Hemingway 100.
49. Hemingway 100.
50. Hemingway 47.
51. Hemingway 54.
52. Hemingway 61.
53. Hemingway 52.
54. Hemingway 53.
55. Hemingway 64.

56. Hemingway 62.
57. Hemingway 61.
58. Hemingway 61.
59. Hemingway 65.
60. Hemingway 61.
61. Hemingway 61.
62. Hemingway 80.
63. Hemingway 80.
64. Hemingway 80.
65. Hemingway 92.
66. Hemingway 92.
67. Hemingway 93.
68. Hemingway 93.
69. Hemingway 94.
70. Hemingway 62.
71. Hemingway 93.
72. Hemingway 93-94.
73. Hemingway 71.
74. C.S. Burhans Jr., '*The Old Man and the Sea*: Hemingway's Tragic Vision of Man,' *American Literature*, XXXI (Jan., 1960), 448.
75. C. Baker, *Hemingway: The Writer as Artist* (Princeton, 1956), 291.
76. Ernest Hemingway, *The Old Man and the Sea* (Moscow, 1967), 100.
77. Hemingway 98.
78. Hemingway 100.
79. Hemingway 102.
80. Hemingway 113.
81. C. Baker (ed.) *Hemingway and His Critics: An International Anthology* (New York, 1961), 255.
82. Ernest Hemingway, *The Old Man and the Sea* (Moscow, 1967), 109.
83. Hemingway 105.
84. Hemingway 47.
85. Hemingway 47.
86. Hemingway 48.
87. Hemingway 49.
88. Hemingway 70.
89. Hemingway 101.

90. Hemingway 10-102.
91. Hemingway 72.
92. Hemingway 102.
93. C.S. Burhans Jr., '*The Old Man and the Sea*: Hemingway's Tragic Vision of Man,' *American Literature*, XXXI (Jan., 1960), 448.
94. Burhans 449.
95. Burhans 449.
96. Ernest Hemingway, *The Old Man and the Sea* (Moscow, 1967), 37-38.
97. Hemingway 57.
98. Hemingway 73.
99. Hemingway 72-73.
100. Hemingway 103.
101. Hemingway 113.
102. Hemingway 113.
103. Hemingway 113.
104. Hemingway 113.
105. C. Baker, *Hemingway: The Writer as Artist* (Princeton, 1956), 291-92.
106. Baker 293.
107. Baker 296.
108. M. Schorer, 'With Grace under Pressure,' *New Republic*, CXXVII (Oct. 6, 1952), 19.
109. J. Waldmeir, 'Confiteor Hominem: Ernest Hemingway's Religion of Man,' Papers of the Michigan Academy of Science, Arts, and Letters, XLII (1957), 349.
110. Waldmeir 350.
111. Waldmeir 350.
112. C. Baker (ed.) *Hemingway and His Critics: An International Anthology* (New Yrok, 1961) 256.
113. Baker 256.
114. Ernest Hemingway, *The Old Man and the Sea* (Moscow, 1967), 34.
115. Hemingway 43.
116. Hemingway 43.
117. Hemingway 58.
118. Hemingway 62.
119. Hemingway 67.
120. Hemingway 35.

121. J. Waldmeir, '*Confiteor Hominem:* Ernest Hemingway's Religion of Man,' Papers of the Michigan Academy of Science, Arts, and Letters, (1957), 350.
122. C. Baker, *Hemingway: The Writer as Artist* (Princeton, 1956), 299.
123. Baker 299.
124. Baker 299.
125. Baker 300.
126. Ernest Hemingway, *The Old Man and the Sea* (Moscow, 1967), 101.
127. Hemingway 75.
128. Hemingway 35.
129. Hemingway 42.
130. Hemingway 44.
131. Hemingway 44.
132. Hemingway 74.
133. Hemingway 74.
134. Hemingway 85.
135. Hemingway 117.
136. C. Baker, *Hemingway: The Writer as Artist* (Princeton, 1956), 306.
137. Baker 304.
138. Baker 304.
139. Ernest Hemingway, *The Old Man and the Sea* (Moscow, 1967), 33.
140. Hemingway 33.
141. Hemingway 33.
142. Hemingway 35.
143. Hemingway 70.
144. Hemingway 70.
145. Hemingway 95.
146. Hemingway 106.
147. Hemingway 84.
148. Hemingway 35.
149. Hemingway 44.
150. Hemingway 44.
151. Hemingway 47.

6

Hemingway's Other Novels and Short Stories

THE MAIN burden of *To Have and Have Not* is the severe hardship that the American economic depression caused to people during the 'thirties. Throughout this novel, Hemingway tries to come out with his acute awareness of the contrast between the rich and the poor, the Haves and the Have Nots. However, this novel in three parts—Part One: Harry Morgan—Spring; Part Two: Harry Morgan—Autumn; and Part Three: Harry Morgan—Winter—is rather clumsy in its execution. The whole of Part One is first-person narrative with Harry Morgan as the narrator; Part Two is in the form of third-person narrative; Chapters I and II of Part Three are told in the first person by Albert Tracy and Harry Morgan respectively, while the remaining sixteen chapters are, once again, in the form of third-person narrative. There is indeed nothing objectionable about these variations or alterations as such: the point of objection is that Hemingway has exercised much less care than they really call for.

To Have and Have Not presents to us a Florida adventurer, Harry Mrgan, as its central character. Like other Hemingway protagonists, Morgan too is a man of action; he does also have courage, resourcefulness, single-mindedness, plenty of endurance and a sense of determination, and yet he is a pig-headed person, a thoughtless man. Aldridge is right when he says that Harry is, no doubt, 'tough..., but has no insides.'[1]

In his book entitled *Cavalcade of the American Novel,* Edward Wagennecht calls *To Have and Have Not* Hemingway's 'worst novel.'[2] In his essay, 'The Background of a Style,' Mark Schorer says:

> The first third of this book is superb narrative in the old manner; but as Hemingway lets himself into the theme proper thereafter, the book begins to break down, and the end is a debacle, the noisy collapse of a style and technique simply unable to support their matter.[3]

And in 'Hemingway's Narrative Perspective,' E.M. Halliday observes:

> In reviewing the almost chaotic technique of *To Have and Have Not*, one is struck by the fact that the technical confusion is matched by a confusion of theme. Harry Morgan, despite his valor, his solid grip on the fundamentals of life, and his splendid domestic virtues, is established in the first section of the book as a thief and murderer, and he remains a curiously unadmirable hero throughout the rest of the story. Moreover, there seems to be some uncertainty about the consistency of Hemingway's intent in attacking such varied representatives of the leisure class as Richard Gordon and Dorothy Hollis, to name only two. The total impression is that of an author groping for his theme in a not-very-well-lighted place, and betrayed into unhappy technical tricks in spasmodic efforts to seize it firmly.[4]

Halliday goes on to say that this novel is 'decidedly mixed in its narrative perspective.'[5] *To Have and Have Not* is indeed a poor, flat novel.

To Have and Have Not has very little of imagery and symbolism in it. Although Part One of this novel offers us some lovely descriptions of fish and fishing and Part Three some beautiful descriptions of Nature, the only symbol which we come across in it is that of sun. In Chapter III of Part One of *To Have and Have Not,* Hemingway presents a picture of the setting sun:

> It was a fine sunset and there was a nice light breeze, and when the sun got pretty well down I started the engine and headed her in slow toward land.[6]

The setting sun stands for Harry Morgan's impending bad luck. Similarly, in Chapter X of the last part of this novel, we come across yet another picture of the evening sun:

> 'Have a drink,' said Harry looking out across the grey swell of Gulf Stream where the round read sun was just touching the water. 'Watch that. When she goes all the way under it'll turn bright green.[7]

This time, we find, the setting sun symbolizes Harry Morgan's imminent death.

As we go through *To Have and Have Not*, we do realize that in this novel Hemingway has not been able to erect an impressive structure of images and symbols in order to be able to convey its theme, or to bring out the emotions or feelings pervading it.

(II) ACROSS THE RIVER AND INTO THE TREES

If *To Have and Have Not* has a mixed narrative perspective, there is nothing mixed in the case of *Across the River and into the Trees*; in fact, this novel contains a narrative told in third person. However, *Across the River and into the Trees* is a disappointing novel. In this connection, in his essay entitled 'Hemingway's Narrative Perspective,' E.M. Halliday says:

> The faults of *Across the River and into the Trees*, for which it has been duly belabored by the reviewers, are not principally matters of narrative perspective. The last days of Colonel Cantwell, an old soldier who refuses to fade away, somehow fail to realize a theme essentially valid and poignant: action inadequate to theme. Between a solid beginning and a solid end we meander through a spongy middle of prolonged conversation wherein the hero expresses to his dream-girl *contessa* numerous prejudices, often malicious and often irrelevant to what meaning the book could have.[8]

Halliday maintains that *Across the River and into the Trees* or whatever kind of action is there in this novel does not do justice to the theme of love and friendship which is sought to be highlighted in the novel against the backdrop of war and anarchy.

A notable capacity for life, a full acceptance and love of the world is always a motivating force with the Hemingway hero, and we do also notice this trait in Colonel Richard Cantwell of *Across the River and into the Trees*. And yet, in spite of flashbacks and interior monologues, or because of them, this novel, artistically speaking, is a failure. Nevertheless, finding an unprecedented display of symbolism in the present novel, Carlos Baker comments that *Across the River and into the Trees* is 'a prose poem, with a remarkably complex emotional structure on the theme of the three ages of man,'[9] and goes on to say that if '*A Farewell to Arms* was his *Romeo and Juliet*...this novel... could perhaps be called a lesser kind of *Winter's Tale* or *Tempest*.'[10]

Hemingway draws the first set of symbols in *Across the River and into the Trees* from Nature, and it is only proper that at the very beginning of this novel he presents a lovely description of a frozen lagoon:

> It was all ice, new-frozen during the windless cold of the night. It was rubbery and bending against the thrust of the boatman's oar.[11]

The canals with bridges over them, the gondolas gliding on their surface, and the wind blowing over the water—all these, besides adding to the beauty of the landscape, symbolize Cantwell's journey to death. In Hemingway's novels, wind and water function as the symbols of a peculiar kind of transformation. In the present novel, besides representing Cantwell's purgation through confession, the wind is also associated with darkness, with cold and high tides, and symbolizes the final cleansing or ablution, that is, death. Likewise, the water of the different canals that Cantwell crosses, strengthens the case of the wind as a symbol, and the gondola moving on the surface of the canal water brings into sharper focus the idea of Cantwell's passage to death.

The various kinds of birds, such as ducks, widgeons, mallards and drakes, that are found all over the lagoon, contribute to the beauty of the landscape and bring out the vitality of life in general. By their very nature or spirit, the trees have their own association with the principle of life. Renata says: 'I like Lombardy poplars and plane trees the best.'[12] In his turn, Cantwell does also like them. He says: 'I like them, and cypresses and chestnut trees. The real chestnut and the horse-chestnut. But you will never see trees, Daughter, until we go to America.'[13] Renata wishes to go to America in order to be able to enjoy the sight of real trees there.

Moreover, the association of emeralds with Renata, with her family and with Venice adds a peculiar charm to these precious stones, and it is not at all difficult to see that they as much symbolize Renata's beauty as the loveliness of the ancient city of Venice. Cantwell touches these stones with his impaired hand; this touch gives him satisfaction, and evokes the memory of all that he had done to defend Venice and Italy. In his essay entitled 'The Structure of Hemingway's *Across the River and into the Trees,*' Peter Lisca says that Richard Cantwell's elaborate narration of his World War experiences acquires the significance of a confession before death.[14] And just as for a quiet death, a reconciliation of opposites, such as love and hate, enmity and friendship, attraction and aversion, is essential, similarly the bridges the Cantwell crosses stand for the opposites to be overcome before his death.

The bridges that Hemingway describes in *Across the River and into the Trees* may be associated with the different stages in Cantwell's life. The first bridge, a temporary one, which Cantwell crosses, may be said to represent the first phase in his encounter with war. The next bridge he crosses may, likewise, be associated with another phase in Cantwell's experience of war. In fact, Hemingway describes several bridges in the novel, and we find that he views them as monuments to soldiers particularly to Cantwell:

> They went under the bridge and under the unfinished wood bridge. Then they left the red bridge on the right and passed under the first high-flying white bridge. Then

> there was the black iron fret-work bridge on the canal.... That's us, he thought. That's our monument. And how many monuments are there to us in the canals of this town?[15]

These bridges over the canals in the city of Venice are associated with the fighting, with the sacrifices made by the soldiers; they are, as Cantwell thinks, the structures raised in the memory of soldiers, both living and dead.

Besides these symbols of wind and water, birds and trees, emeralds and bridges in *Across the River and into the Trees*, we do also come across several other images and symbols in this novel that have their own meaningfulness. The bodies of the dead, all 'floating and bloating'[16] in the canals, as Cantwell recollects them, stand for the cruelty, the catastrophic aspect of war. The body of a dead soldier flattened on the road by the moving vehicles and of a dead phosphorous-roasted German, being eaten first by a dog and then by a cat, represent the destruction and chaos unleashed by war. Similarly, the very picture of the aeroplanes of the Allied Powers bombing their own soldiers by mistake does symbolize the nervousness and desperation of the combatants in certain cases.

The reference to a highway and a secondary road in the present novel do also have their own suggestiveness. Richard Cantwell's driver, Jackson, is afraid of driving on a secondary road. 'Say, Jackson,' speaks Cantwell, 'do you always suffer so much any time you go off a highway on to a secondary road?'[17] Jackson's hesitation symbolizes the adoption of no line other than the traditional one, for here is a driver who cannot innovate or take new risks as Cantwell does.

The impaired engine of the boat that Cantwell hires, makes sound like that of 'a stricken tank,'[18] and does immediately remind us of the Colonel's diseased and weak heart. The engine's 'metallic agony that produced a slight increase in speed'[19] suggests what Cantwell's heart can achieve only after sustained effort. Cantwell is indeed conscious of the fact that every move the damaged engine makes is 'a triumph of the gallantry of the ageing machine,'[20] and, quite naturally, he thinks of his own heart: 'I do not see why, that one, of all the muscles, should fail me.'[21] The engine's 'metallic agony' points directly to the occasional 'twinges'[22] of Cantwell's heart, and suggests his impending death.

In *Across the River and into the Trees,* even a hotel or a bar is made to represent what Hemingway understands by home. Characteristically enough, Renata's presence adds considerably to the homelike quality of a hotel. It is really interesting to see that the play of light on the ceiling of the hotel, reflected from the water of the canal, makes it a clean, well-lighted place where *nada* cannot prevail. In fact, Renata'a company can transform even a gondola into an image of home. Renata tells Richard Cantwell: 'We are in our home and I love you.'[23] And just as in Hemingway's novels, particularly in *Across the River and into the Trees* and *For Whom the Bell Tolls*, long hair serves as a symbol of womanhood,[24] similarly, Cantwell's impaired hand works as a symbol, as a religious symbol. Renata is always desirous of touching it and feeling it. She says: 'I wanted to feel it because all last week, every night, or I think nearly every night, I dreamed about it and it was a strange mix-up dream and I dreamed it was the hand of Our Lord.'[25] The very touch and feel of this hand gives Renata a curious satisfaction.

Across the River and into the Trees contains the story of a dying American Colonel's last love affair in Venice, and in this respect it is often compared with Thomas Mann's long short story entitled *Death in Venice*. However, this comparison, in a way, harms Hemingway's case as an artist. *Death in Venice* is a brilliant psychological study of an ageing writer, and the Venetian atmosphere, pervading the story, lends it a peculiar kind of charm. Hemeingway's Colonel Richard Cantweel is a disillusioned man, full of bitterness, sick at heart, who tries to recapture his youth in the company of a young Italian countess. The present novel has no perspective, either intellectual, psychological, or artistic. Howsoever enthusiastic Carlos Baker may be in speaking about the nature of symbolism in *Across the River and into the Trees*, the fact remains that this novel offers only a poor picture as compared with *The Sun Also Rises*, *A Farewell to Arms, For Whom the Bell Tolls*, and *The Old Man and the Sea* on the symbolic level.

(III) ISLANDS IN THE STREAM

Islands in the Stream, a posthumously-published novel in three parts (Part I: Bimini; Part II: Cuba; Part III: At Sea), deals basically with Thomas Hudson's predicament, with his physical problems and psychic complexities. Hudson is a painter, a devoted painter, and he has his idyllic house on the seacoast in Bimini. 'His life,' says Hemingway, 'was built solidly on work and on the living by the Gulf Stream and on the Island and it would stand up all right.'[26] The novelist adopts the third-person narrative technique in his present work, but he brings in variations in this technique by introducing flashbacks in this novel from time to time.

The most important and outstanding symbol in *Islands in the Stream* is that of the sea. It is a magnetic, all-pervading presence in the novel, and, in a way, it forms the background as well as the foreground of this work. Nevertheless, as we go through the present novel, we do come to realize that Hemingway is extremely fond of the Gulf Stream which, as it were, at the centre of the sea, its very heart, and which keeps the sea in motion by virtue of its flow and the life associated with it. Moreover, the Gulf Stream stands for extraordinary and strange depths as well as for a distance that is generally out of the reach of common people. Thus, the sea-Gulf Stream complex symbolizes the universe, the infinite cosmos, the manifest creation and the principle of life governing it. And this is how we may best try to explain the burden of the present novel's title.

It is not without significance that Hemingway describes the cycle of seasons in *Islands in the Stream*. 'After one has lived in those latitudes long enough, the changes of seasons become as important there as anywhere else and Thomas Hudson, who loved the island, did not want to miss any spring, nor any summer, nor any fall nor winter.'[27] The Gulf is not always a picture of the pleasant or the amiable; it has its storms, its hurricanes, its sharks, its changing moods, and it is dark and deep and unfathomable. The sea is, thus, not merely a symbol of good, peace, or order, it is also a symbol of evil, sorrow, or chaos in the universe. The sea does not help Hudson's team in pursuing the Germans, because the eastern wind has started blowing and the water of the channel has receded, resulting in the grounding of Hudson's ship. Similarly, the rains which, in Hemingway's novels, do always symbolize complication, obstruct all military adventures.

REFERENCES

1. J.W. Aldridge, *After the Lost Generation* (New York, 1951), 32.
2. E. Wagenknecht, *Cavalcade of the American Novel* (Calcutta, 1952), 377.
3. M. Schorer, 'The Background of a Style,' *Kenyon Review* III (Winter, 1941), 101.
4. E.M. Halliday, 'Hemingway's Narrative Perspective,' *Sewanee Review*, IX (Spring, 1952), 214.
5. Halliday 202.
6. Ernest Hemingway, *To Have and Have Not* (Penguin edition, 1969), 41.
7. Hemingway 128.
8. E.M. Halliday, 'Hemingway's Narrative Perspective,' *Sewanee Review*, LX (Spring, 1952), 216-17.
9. C. Baker, *Hemingway: The Writer as Artist* (Princeton, 1956), 264.
10. Baker 287.
11. Ernest Hemingway, *Across the River and into the Trees* (Penguin edition, 1966), 5.
12. Hemingway 159.
13. Hemingway 159.
14. See P. Lisca, *The Structure of Hemingway's Across the River and into the Trees*, *Modern Fiction Studies* (Summer, 1966), 248.
15. Ernest Hemingway, *Across the River and into the Trees* (Penguin edition, 1966), 38.

16. Hemingway 19.
17. Hemingway 21.
18. Hemingway 36.
19. Heminway 38.
20. Hemingway 43.
21. Hemingway 93.
22. Hemingway 63.
23. Hemingway 118.
24. Hemingway 85-86.
25. Hemingway 67.
26. Ernest Hemingway, *Islands in the Stream* (Bantam Books, 1971), 91.
27. *Ibid*.

7
Conclusion

SPEAKING OF symbolism and irony together in his very illuminating essay entitled 'Hemingway's Ambiguity: Symbolism and Irony,' E.M. Halliday says:

> ...all perceptions are reducible finally to perception of likeness or perceptions of difference. Perhaps this offers a clue to the effectiveness of both symbolism and irony.... Symbolism does depend essentially on likeness, and irony on difference; and as artistic tools both are means of interpreting imaginatively, and with the flexibility of implication, a complex reality. Symbolism signifies through a harmony, irony through a discord; symbolism consolidates, irony complicates; symbolism sythesizes, irony analyzes.[1]

Halliday does rightly point out that symbolism depends on the likeness of two or more than two objects, that it is a mode of perception, that as an artistic tool it seeks to interpret complex realities imaginatively, and that it works through harmony and synthesis.

It is in the context of Hemingway's use of images and symbols in his fictional works that we have to refer to what is known as his Iceberg theory of language and presentation. In *Death in the Afternoon,* Hemingway writes:

> If a writer of prose known enough about what he is writing about he may omit things that he knows and the reader, if the writer is writing truly enough, will have a feeling of those things as strongly as though the writer had stated them. The dignity of movement of an iceberg is due to only one-eighth of it being above water.[2]

No doubt, Hemingway is a realist; no doubt, he maintains strict fidelity to realism, to the truthfulness of details and descriptions, and yet we find that his imagination, his artistic invention yields a kind of truth that is much higher than or superior to the realism or truthfulness of factual account. Carlos Baker speaks of the artist's 'grasp of the relationship between the temporal and the eternal,'[3] and says that this 'grasp is expressed, in his fiction, through the considered use of imaginative symbols.'[4] With particular reference to Hemingway, Baker goes on to say:

> Most of these come, by way of the artist's imagination, from the visible material universe—the mountains and the plains, the rivers and the trees, the weather and the seasons, the land and the sea. To such natural images Hemingway has attached the strong emotional power of his artistic apprehension of them.... At the same time, Hemingway has generally managed to render with fidelity each of the natural objects or scenes precisely for what, in itself, it really is. As a result of their union with imagination and emotion, the various phenomena rise up as operative symbols in all his art. They become thereby not less real but more real than they are in themselves because of the double or triple significations with which they have been imbued.[5]

There is indeed a peculiarly productive combination of the real and the imaginative, of realism and symbolism, of fact and suggestion, of statement and implication in Hemingway's novels.

II

As we have said earlier, Ernest Hemingway is remembered both as a writer and legend, for in his case the two are nearly inseparable from each other. Hemingway was a prolific writer, and even though he was not very much interested in formal education, he had started writing and contributing to journals while he was just a seventeen-year old boy and a student at the Oak Park School. It is true that he did have a great passion for sports and outdoor activities, and yet it seems that he had decided rather early in his life to take to writing as a vocation. And it is towards this end that he made sustained efforts to learn as much from the world of letters as from his direct encounter with life. His career as a journalist, spread over a large span of time, that took him to various important places in America and Europe, his defiant and persistent participation in wars and revolutions, his close association with the Paris literary circle, his anti-Fascist stance, his first-hand experience of human suffering and of the loss of traditional values in a world ravaged by wars, and his penchant for recording his impressions and experience in the form of fictional narrative—all these drove Hemingway into adopting a course that helped him in shaping himself as a writer of fiction. It is no wonder, then, that, besides others, he wrote such great fictional works as *The Sun Also Rises, A Farewell to Arms, For Whom the Bell Tolls,* and *The Old Man and the Sea.*

It may not be very profitable to discuss the nature and magnitude of influences that might have worked on Hemingway, for he is the one great American writer who belongs to no known school or tradition of fiction. And still, as we have said earlier, we cannot do without referring, in the first place, to Hemingway's adverse reaction to the rather conservative and puritanical ambience of Oak Park, to his sense of dilemma over the war of nerves that went on and on between his father and his mother and his predilection for his father in respect of the latter's passion for fishing, swimming and hunting, to the wholesome training Hemingway received at the hands of two of his Oak Park School teachers, Miss Gibbs and Miss Dixon, and to the inspiration he imbibed, even as a boy, from Rudyard Kipling and Ring Lardner. Secondly, as a journalist working with the Kansas City *Star,* he was greatly influenced by C.G. Wellington and Lionel Calhourn Moise who persistently guided him in the art of writing and encouraged him to keep on improving his composition. Yet another journalist who inspired him considerably was William Bolitho Ryall, for he 'strengthened in Hemingway his knowledgeability, his instinct for being on the inside, and his insistence that one should think for himself.'[6] Thirdly, if Hemingway was not happy during his stay in Chicago for a brief journalistic stint there on account of what he viewed as American commercialism and American insensitivity to human suffering, he was not close to Sherwood Anderson either. And yet, as we have pointed out earlier, in a certain way Anderson did influence Hemingway. Fourthly, during his stay in Paris, Hemingway learnt a good deal, among others, from Gertrude Stein and Ezra Pound who advised him to take up his literary pursuits seriously, and, as a first step towards this, to give up journalism. And finally, it was Hemingway's experiences and impressions of wars and revolutions, of World War I, Graeco-Turkish War, Spanish Civil War and World War II, that affected him to a substantial degree.

Nevertheless, Hemingway was perhaps too independent a writer to accept any influence or influences completely, and naturally we have to consider him as a writer of fiction in his own right.

Ernest Hemingway has been read and is still being read widely, and a good deal has been written on his mind and art, on the basic theme of his writings, on his narrative technique, on his characters, on his prose style, and on the ambiguity in his fiction. However, it is so very easy to see that Hemingway's reputation does register a sharp curve, either upward or downward, and that while a number of scholars and critics look upon his fictional writings as meaningful, profound and well-executed literary exercises, there are others who find him only cheap, superficial, and rather addicted to sensationalism. What is obviously required is a patient, thorough and balanced assessment of Hemingway's fictional art.

III

As we have noted earlier, considered as a work of fiction, *The Sun Also Rises* may seem to be 'a slight thing;'[7] at times we may tend to discard it as an immoral book[8] chiefly for the reason that the world of this novel is one of drunken promiscuity, and yet we cannot and should not lose sight of the fact that Hemingway did have his own concern for the meaning and values of human life, that his is 'an intensely implicational'[9] mode of writing in spite of his austere and sparse style, that his novels do contain 'submerged'[10] meanings, and that his images function as the 'symbols of an inner world.'[11] Mark Spilka says the very same thing in a different way when he states that 'with Hemingway, the great outdoors is chiefly a state of mind, a projection of moral and emotional attitudes on to physical arenas, so that a clear account of surface action will reproduce these attitudes in the reader.'[12]

As we have said earlier, it is for quite understandable reasons that we come across images of emptiness in *The Sun Also Rises;* however, it is also equally understandable that these images of emptiness are generally followed by those of cleansing; mopping up, or sweeping. Similarly, quite a few of the other images that we get in the present novel relate chiefly to the false knight, Robert Cohn, though there are some that take us straight on to the bull-fighter, Pedro Romero. We have also discussed at some length the importance of such images in *The Sun Also Rises* as present to us a picture of happiness, growth and fruitfulness amidst despair, decay and degeneration. It is in this light that we have to interpret the goat image and the images pertaining to bull-fight and fishing that we get in this novel.

At this point, it is important to refer to the suggestiveness of some of the symbols—the symbol of rain, of the game of poker dice, of a mounted policeman directing traffic, of Brett Ashley's trembling hands, and the symbol of the scars of arrow wounds on the Count's back in particular—that we get in *The Sun Also Rises.* We have also considered the present novel as a parable, as an extended parable in fact, in which images and symbols do have their own value. At the same time, we have also tried to bring out the allegorical significance of the title of this novel, which has been taken from *Ecclesiastes* of *The Old Testament* and which suggests that though all is vanity, vanity of vanities really, the earth abides for ever.

A Farewell to Arms may be explained, as is usually done, in realistic terms, for, besides other things, it does deal with the effect of war on human life, with what happened to a small group of people on the Italian front during 1917-18. This novel may also be interpreted as a work of fiction that seeks to draw our attention, as James F. Light says, to 'the four ideals of service.'[13] He observes:

> Each of these ideals is dramatized by a character of some importance, and it is between these four that Lt. Henry wavers in the course of the novel. The orthodoxy religious ideal of service is that of the priest.... Another selfless ideal of service is that of the partriot Gino.... A third is the code of Catherine Barkley who wishes to serve her lover and who *sees* in such service her personal substitute for conventional religion. The last is the ideal of Rinaldi who, as a doctor, wishes to serve mankind by alleviating the wounds of war.[14]

However, this idealistic stance of the book may not preclude our looking at it in terms of its ironic suggestiveness. E.M. Halliday observes: 'the ironic gap between expectation and fulfillment, pretense and fact, intention and action, the message sent and the message received, the way things are thought or ought to be and the way things are—this has been Hemingway's great theme from the beginning; and it has called for an ironic method to do it artistic justice.'[15]

Nevertheless, its realism, its supposed commitment to idealism, or its ironic mode of presentation 'ought not finally to obscure the symbolic mythos on which *A Farewell to Arms* is built and from which a great part of its emotional power derives.'[16]

Some of the more important symbols—the symbol of rain, of the dust, of the fallen and falling leaves, of the river, of the log of wood, full of ants, on top of the fire—that we have explained in the preceding pages form part of the weather or nature symbolism which is indeed so very vital for the texture of this novel. And some of the major images—the image of the game of chess and of bridge, the image of a dog in heat, the image of arrival after a long trip, the image of cemetery and of the worn carpet, the image of empty cans and saucers, the image of the

Inquisition and the image of a statue—do substantially contribute to the symbolical make-up of *A Farewell to Arms.*

At this point, as we have discussed earlier, we cannot do without referring to 'the central antithesis between the image of life, love, and home (the mountain) and the image of war and death (the plain)'[17] which Carlos Baker explains in so great a detail and in which, according to him, Catherine has 'a symbolic part to play.'[18]

A Farewell to Arms is indeed a highly symbolical novel, and we have to consider it as such. In fact, it is a dexterous combination of realism and symbolism that accounts for the success of this novel as a work of art.

In his comments on *For Whom the Bell Tolls,* Carlos Baker identifies the 'elements of the epic manner'[19] that Hemingway adapts to his needs in this novel, and in this connection observes:

> Despite the obvious gap between Spain and Ilium, the student of the epic may find part of his answer in considering the Homeric parallel. A primitive setting, simple food and wine, the care and use of weapons, the sense of imminent danger, the emphasis on masculine prowess, the presence of varying degrees of courage and cowardice, the rude barbarisms on both sides, the operation of certain religious and magical superstitions, the warrior codes—these, surely, are common ties between the two sets of protagonists. Jordan is not to be scorned as the type of Achilles, and one can recognize in Pablo the rude outlines of a debased and sulking Ajax. Pilar the gypsy, though she reads the lifeline in Jordan's palm instead of consulting the shape and color of animal entrails, makes the consciousness of the supernatural an operative factor.[20]

Moreover, Baker does also refer to 'the intentionally heightened language'[21] that Hemingway adopts in the present novel.

We may or may not accept *For Whom the Bell Tolls* as an epic of sorts, but we can hardly be unmindful of the novel's shortcomings. Pilar's narration of the story of the massacre of the Fascists in Chapter 10 of the novel does not seem to be quite justified, even though it seeks to glorify Pablo who is now merely a cowardly ghost of his former brave and determined self. Similarly, we find ourselves somewhat reluctant to accept several chapters of the novel, particularly Chapters 26, 30 and 34, that contain almost intermindable and tiring ruminations. Moreover, at times we do have a feeling that what this novel offers us is more of a Robert Jordan-Maria love story than anything else. And lastly, at least in patches, this novel strikes us as a routine sentimental exercise. As we have observed earlier, the conversation that goes on between the wounded Robert Jordan and the anxiety-ridden Maria, gives us a taste of sentimental effusion.[22]

Nevertheless, *For Whom the Bell Tolls* is a highly symbolical novel, and it is only proper to examine it as such.

The title of this novel has been taken from one of John Donne's meditations, part of which is available to us as its epigraph. Though the stress in the novel's epigraph is on the theme of human solidarity, somehow or other Hemingway has not been able to drive this point home to us, with the result that he seems to be promoting the cause or cult of alienated individualism. The controversy about the novel in this regard is quite understandable.

However, the first important and outstanding symbol in *For Whom the Bell Tolls* is that of the bridge that Robert Jordan has to blow up for the Republican cause. It is worth noting that the word 'bridge' occurs for 294 times in the novel, and that while this word occurs for 32 times in Chapter I of the novel, it is used for 110 times in the last chapter of this book. As a symbol, the bridge stands for freedom, for hope for the future of human race itself. Maria's hair, her growing hair in fact, serves as the next important symbol in the present novel. Maria, as her very name implies may be associated with the Virgin, but she is a 'violated virgin,'[23] for the Fascists have tortured and raped her and have got her head shaved mercilessly time and again. The loss of her hair suggests the loss of normal womanhood, while its gradual growth implies Maria's gradual return to balance and health.

As we have said earlier, the contrast between Republicanism and Fascism, between freedom and dictatorship, between man and machine, between the primitive society and the technological civilization, between Nature and the bombers that Hemingway offers in *For Whom the Bell Tolls* does have its own symbolic implications. And it is in this very light that we do also have to interpret the sport of bull-fight to which references are made in the novel, for, besides being a typical Spanish sport, the bull-fight represents man's heroism, his masculine prowess, his capacity for endurance. Similarly, the wheel symbol in the present novel suggests neither a wheel for a joy-ride nor the conventionally-accepted wheel of fortune; instead, as we have already pointed out, it suggests the wheel of human conflict.

The other two symbols that compel our attention in *For Whom the Bell Tolls* are Velazquez 63 and Gaylordś. Velazquez 63 is the headquarters of the International Brigade, and it symbolizes the puritanical, austere and ritualistic kind of Communism that is taught and practised there. On the other hand, the Madrid hotel, Gaylordś, represents a kind of Communism that is based on conceit, deceitfulness and betrayal.

It is important to remember that the Fascist planes fly either in threes or in the formations of three, and that three is supposed to be a magical or mystical number. Similarly, the frequent use of the term *nada,* meaning *nothing* or *nothingness*, in the present novel suggests something sinister that is going to invade, disturb or destroy Spain's primitive culture and earthiness. And, as we have noted earlier rather in detail, the odour image that we come across in *For Whom the Bell Tolls* does have its own profound meaningfulness. In fact, almost all the images that Hemingway draws either from Nature or from the field of science do have their own appropriateness and appeal.

At the same time, it is also equally important to remember that almost all the major characters we encounter in the present novel are, in one way or another, closely connected with the bridge. The Chief of the demolition squad, Robert Jordan who is also the hero of the novel, is the very symbol of human freedom and dignity; Anselmo stands for a strict commitment to duty in spite of his severe hatred for violence; Rafael represents irresponsible paganism; Pablo is a veritable Judas, a symbol of the canker of defeatism, one who is afraid to die; Pilar, in spite of all her faults, is an archetypal Mother, the very image of primitivism, compassion and courage, while Maria symbolizes a longing for home.

In his essay entitled 'Hemingway's Ambiguity: Symbolism and Irony,' E.M. Halliday observes that 'the sleeping bag in *For Whom the Bell Tolls* is an obvious symbol of the womb.'[24] It is difficult to say anything else about Robert Jordan's sleeping bag, for it is inside this sleeping bag that the American dynamiter and Maria make love.

For Whom the Bell Tolls contains a large number of symbols and images, and we can understand and appreciate the novel to the desired extent only if and when we comprehend the implications of these symbols and images.

A close and careful study of *The Old Man and the Sea* gives us a definite impression of the fact that here is a novel, the scope of which is not just limited to a presentation of realistic details about an old fisherman's desperate and protracted struggle with a huge fish and the sharks; instead, we do realize that here is a novel which is indeed a successful work of art, poetic, symbolical, full of images, and ambiguous in a rich and positive sense. As we have seen earlier, Santiago is not merely the symbol of strength, endurance and determination, he does also stand for love and affection, pride and humility, piety and compassion. There are enough hints in the novel to suggest that Santiago is a Christ-like figure, that his suffering and nobility do constitute what we may call the phenomenon of Crucifixion, and that the novel does have its own Christian or religious association. Moreover, there are two qualities in his character, his heroic individualism and his patience, that remind us necessarily of Job. Similarly, the huge fish, Santiago's prize catch, is not only the marvel of creation, it is also something akin to Christ, for, as we have pointed out earlier, fish has been traditionally associated with Christ. The next symbol that deserves mention at this point comes to us in the form of the sharks which represent the forces of death and destruction. In its own turn, the sea with all its depth and vastness, symbolizes both mystery and immensity, and Santiago's feeling of loneliness during his drift on the sea is quite natural and understandable.

As we have said earlier, the boy, Manolin, is Santiago's disciple, and the relationship between the boy and the old fisherman is that between the taught and his teacher, between a son and his adopted father. However, the boy in the novel is a symbol of the old fisherman's remembrance of his youth, of his craving for immortality, and it is no wonder that from time to time during his days of loneliness and stress, Santiago wishes the boy to be with himself. Likewise, the old fisherman's occasional dreams relating to Africa and its lions are a symbolic pointer to his strength and tenacity during his youth. These dreams, we have said, serve the purpose of a psychological stimulus to Santiago; they are a sort of wish-fulfilment, a kind of compensation for what he has not been able to achieve in life. Similarly, the baseball player, DiMaggio, is Santiago's favourite; the old fisherman speaks of him or remembers him at several places in the novel, and he uses the word 'great' almost repeatedly for him. These references to DiMaggio reflect not only Santiago's passion for the baseball game, they do also heighten his feeling for teamwork, for solidarity, for human interdependence at a time when he is all alone on the sea, facing the challenge of his grim encounter with the fish and the sharks.

It is important to remember that Santiago, a name that takes us to Saint James, a fisherman, apostle and martyr from the Sea of Galilee, is the central symbol in *The Old Man and the Sea* and that all the other symbols of this novel revolve round this very central symbol.

To Have and Have Not has very little of imagery and symbolism in it. Although Part One of this novel offers us some lovely descriptions of fish and fishing and Part Three some beautiful descriptions of Nature, the only symbol which we come across in it is that of sun. In Chapter III of Part One of *To Have and Have Not,* Hemingway presents a picture of the setting sun:

> It was a fine sunset and there was a nice light breeze, and when the sun got pretty well down I started the engine and headed her in slow toward land.[25]

The setting sun stands for Harry Morgan's impending bad luck. Similarly, in Chapter X of the last part of this novel we come across yet another picture of the evening sun:

> 'Have a drink,' said Harry looking out across the grey swell of the Gulf Stream where the round red sun was just touching the water. 'Watch that when she goes all the way under it'll turn bright green.'[26]

This time, we find, the setting sun symbolizes Harry Morgan's imminent death.

As we go through *To Have and Have Not*, we do realize that in this novel Hemingway has not been able to erect an impressive structure of images and symbols in order to be able to convey its theme, or to bring out the emotions or feelings pervading it.

Hemingway draws the first set of symbols in *Across the River and into the Trees* from Nature, and it is only proper that at the very beginning of this novel he presents a lovely description of a frozen lagoon:

> It is all ice, new-frozen during the windless cold of the night. It was rubbery and bending against the thrust of boatman's oar.[27]

The canals with bridges over them, the gondolas gliding on their surface, and the wind blowing over the water—all these, besides adding to the beauty of the landscape, symbolize Cantwell's journey to death. In Hemingway's novels, wind and water function as the symbols of a peculiar kind of transformation. In the present novel, besides representing Cantwell's purgation through confession, the wind is also associated with darkness, with cold and high tides, and symbolizes the final cleansing or ablution, that is, death. Likewise, the water of the different canals that Cantwell crosses, strengthens the case of the wind as a symbol, and the gondola moving on the surface of the canal water brings into sharper focus the idea of Cantwell's passage to death.

The various kinds of birds, such as ducks, widgeons, mallards and drakes, that are found all over the lagoon, contribute to the beauty of the landscape and bring out the vitality of life in general. By their very nature or spirit, the trees have their own association with the principle of life. Renata says: 'I like Lombardy poplars and plane trees the best.'[28] In his turn, Cantwell does also like them. He says: 'I like them, and cypresses and chestnut trees. The real chestnut and the horse-chestnut. But you will never see trees, Daughter, until we go to America.'[29] Renata wishes to go to America in order to be able to enjoy the sight of real trees there.

Moreover, the association of emeralds with Renata, with her family and with Venice adds a peculiar charm to these precious stones, and it is not at all difficult to see that they as much symbolize Renata's beauty as the loveliness of the ancient city of Venice. Cantwell touches these stones with his impaired hand; this touch gives him satisfaction, and evokes the memory of all that he had done to defend Venice and Italy. In his essay entitled 'The Structure of Hemingway's *Across the River and into the Trees,*' Peter Lisca says that Richard Cantwell's elaborate narration of his Wold War experiences acquires the significance of a confession before death.[30] And just as for a quiet death a reconciliation of opposites, such as love and hate, enmity and friendship, attraction and aversion, is essential, similarly the bridges that Cantwell crosses stand for the opposites to be overcome before his death.

The bridges that Hemingway describes in *Across the River and into the Tress* may be associated with the different stages in Cantwell's life. The first bridge, a temporary one, which Cantwell crosses, may be said to represent the first phase in his encounter with war. The next bridge he crosses may, likewise, be associated with another phase in Cantwell's experience of war. In fact, Hemingway describes several bridges in the novel, and we find that he views them as monuments to soldiers, particularly to Cantwell:

> They went under bridge and under the unfinished woodbridge. Then they left the red bridge on the right and passed under the first high-flying white bridge. Then there was the black iron fret-work bridge on the canal.... That's us, he thought. That's our monument. And how many monuments are there to us in the canals of this town?[31]

These bridges over the canals in the city of Venice are associated with the fighting, with the sacrifices made by the soldiers; they are, as Cantwell thinks, the structures raised in the memory of soldiers, both living and dead.

Besides these symbols of wind and water, birds and trees, emeralds and bridges in *Across the River and into the Trees*, we do also come across several other images and symbols in this novel that have their own meaningfulness. The bodies of the dead, all 'floating and bloating'[32] in the canals, as Cantwell recollects them, stands for the cruelty, the catastrophic aspect of war. The body of a dead soldier flattened on the road by the moving vehicles and of a dead phosphorous-roasted German, being eaten first by a dog and then by a cat, represent the destruction and chaos unleashed by war. Similarly, the very picture of the aeroplanes of the Allied Powers bombing their own soldiers by mistake does symbolize the nervousness and desperation of the combatants in certain cases.

The references to a highway and a secondary road in the present novel do also have their own suggestiveness. Richard Cantwell's driver, Jackson, is afraid of driving on a secondary road. 'Say, Jackson,' speaks Cantwell, 'do you always suffer so much any time you go off a highway on to a secondary road?'[33] Jackson's hesitation symbolizes the adoption of no line other than the traditional one, for here is driver who cannot innovate or take new risks as Cantwell does.

The impaired engine of the boat that Cantwell hires, makes sound like that of 'a stricken tank,'[34] and does immediately remind us of the Colonel's diseased and weak heart. The engine's 'metallic agony that produced a slight increase in speed'[35] suggests that Cantwell's heart can achieve only after sustained effort. Cantwell is indeed conscious of the fact that every move the damaged engine makes is 'a triumph of the gallantry of the ageing machine,'[36] and, quite naturally, he thinks of his own heart: 'I do not see why, that one, of all the muscles, should fail me.'[37] The engine's 'metallic agony' points directly to the occasional 'twinges'[38] of Cantwell's heart, and suggests his impending death.

In *Across the River and into the Trees,* even a hotel or a bar is made to represent what Hemingway understands by home. Characteristically enough, Renata's presence adds considerably to the homelike quality of a hotel. It is really interesting to see that the play of light on the ceiling of the hotel, reflected from the water of the canal, makes it a clean, well-lighted place where *nada* cannot prevail. In fact, Renata's company can transform even a gondola into an image of home. Renata tells Richard Cantwell: 'We are in our home and I love you.'[39] And just as in Hemingway's novels, particularly in *Across the River and into the Trees* and *For Whom the Bell Tolls*, long hair serves as a symbol of woman-hood,[40] similarly, Cantwell's impaired hand works as a symbol, as a religious symbol. Renata is always desirous of touching it and feeling it. She says: 'I wanted to feel it because all last week, every night, or I think nearly every night, I dreamed about it and it was a strange mix-up dream and I dreamed it was the hand of Our Lord.'[41] The very touch and feel of this hand gives Renata a curious satisfaction.

Across the River and into the Trees contains the story of a dying American Colonel's last love affair in Venice, and in this respect it is often compared with Thomas Mann's long short story entitled *Death in Venice*. However, this comparison, in a way, harms Hemingway's case as an artist. *Death in Venice* is a brilliant psychological study of an ageing writer, and the Venetian atmosphere, pervading the story, lends it a peculiar kind of charm. Hemingway's Colonel Richard Cantwell is a disillusioned man, full of bitterness, sick at heart, who tries to recapture his youth in the company of a young Italian countess. The present novel has no perspective, either intellectual, psychological, or artistic. Howsoever enthusiastic Carlos Baker may be in speaking about the nature of symbolism in *Across the River and into the Trees,* the fact remains that his novel offers only a poor picture as compared with *The Sun Also Rises*, *A Farewell to Arms, For Whom the Bell Tolls*, and *The Old Man and the Sea* on the symbolic level.

The most important and outstanding symbol in *Islands in the Stream* is that of the sea. It is a magnetic, all-pervading presence in the novel; in a way, it forms the background as well as the foreground of this work. Nevertheless, as we go through the present novel, we do come to realize that Hemingway is extremely fond of the Gulf Stream which is, as it were, at the centre of the sea, its very heart, and which keeps the sea in motion by virtue of its flow and the life associated with it. Moreover, the Gulf Stream stands for extraordinary and strange depths as well as for a distance that is generally out of the reach of common people. Thus, the Sea-Gulf Stream complex symbolizes the universe, the infinite cosmos, the manifest creation and the principle of life governing it. And this is how we may best try to explain the burden of the present novel's title.

It is not without significance that Hemingway describes the cycle of seasons in *Islands in the Stream.* 'After one has lived on those latitudes long enough, the changes of seasons become as important there as anywhere else and Thomas Hudson, who loved the island, did not want to miss any spring, nor any summer, nor any fall nor winter.'[42] The Gulf is not always a picture of the pleasant or the amiable; it has its storms, its hurricanes, it sharks, its changing moods, and it is dark and deep and unfathomable. The sea is, thus, not merely a symbol of good, peace, or order, it is also a symbol of evil, sorrow, or chaos in the universe. The sea does not help Hudson's team in pursuing the Germans, because the eastern wind has started blowing and the water of the channel has receded, resulting in the grounding of Hudson's ship. Similarly, the rains which, in Hemingway's novels, do always symbolize complication, obstruct all military adventures.

Whatever symbols are there in *Islands in the Stream*, all that they do or are intended to do is to bring out the unpredictability or inscrutability of the sea, the real, life-giving motion of the Gulf Stream, and the principles of life and death, creation and destruction, good and evil that govern the course of what is known as the manifest universe.

IV

It is worthwhile to mention that there has been a gradual revolution of symbolism in Heningway's novels. As we go through his first novel entitled *The Sun Also Rises*, we find that in it symbols and images do not play as crucial or vital role as they do in his second major novel captioned *A Farewell to Arms*. It is so very plain to see that the symbols and images in *A Farewell to Arms* far outnumber those in *The Sun Also Rises*. As we move still further, we do notice a distinctly heavy preponderance of symbols and images in the next two of Hemingway's major novels named *For Whom the Bell Tolls* and *The Old Man and the Sea*. It appears that in a very patient manner Hemingway cultivated the art of introducing symbols and images in his novels. As we have stated earlier, a large number of these symbols and images may be traced to nature: quite a few of them have been borrowed from religion, while rest of them owe their origin to other fields of human activity. At this point, it is both interesting and profitable to refer to Hemingway's iceberg theory of stylistic technique, about which so much has been said in the preceding pages. Lastly, we just cannot do without recalling the fact that while on the one hand Hemingway is a realist, on the other he is a symbolist, and that both realism and symbolism co-exist and reinforce each other in his novels. In any case, symbolism adds a very refreshing and rich dimension to his novels.

REFERENCES

1. E.M. Halliday, 'Hemingway's Ambiguity: Symbolism and Irony,' *American Literature,* xxvii (March, 1956), 22.
2. Ernest Hemingway, *Death in the Afternoon* (New York, 1932), 183.
3. C. Baker, *Hemingway: The Writer as Artist* (Princeton, 1956), 289.
4. Baker 289-90.
5. Baker 290.
6. C.A. Fenton, *The Apprenticeship of Ernest Hemingway* (New York, 1954), 195.
7. E. Wagenknecht, *Cavalcade of the American Novel* (Calcutta, 1952), 369.
8. Wagenknecht 375.
9. Wagenknecht 372.
10. See George Hemphill, 'Hemingway and James,' *Kenyon Review,* XI (1949), 50-60.
11. See Introduction to Malcolm Cowley, *Ernest Hemingway: The Man and His Work* (New York, 1944), 316-17.
12. C. Shapiro (ed.) *Twelve Original Essays on Great American Novels* (Detroit, 1958), 245.
13. J.F. Light, 'The Religion of Death in *A Farewell to Arms*,' *Modern Fiction Studies,* VII (Summer, 1961), 169.
14. Light 169.
15. E.M. Halliday, 'Hemingway's Ambiguity: Symbolism and Irony,'*American Literature,* xxviii (March, 1956), 15.
16. C. Baker, *Hemingway: The Writer as Artist* (Princeton, 1956), 116.
17. Baker 116.
18. Baker 116.
19. Baker 248.
20. Baker 248.
21. Baker 248.
22. See E. Hemingway, *For Whom the Bell Tolls* (Penguin edition, 1964), 436.
23. See Melvin Backman, 'Hemingway: The Matador and the Crucified,' *Modern Fiction Studies,* 1 (August, 1955), 7.
24. E.M. Halliday, 'Hemingway's Ambiguity: Symbolism and Irony,' *American Literature,* xxviii (March, 1956), 4.
25. Ernest Hemingway, *To Have and Have Not* (Penguin edition, 1969), 41.
26. Hemingway128.

27. Ernest Hemingway, *Across the River and into the Trees* (Penguin edition, 1966), 5.
28. Hemingway 159.
29. Hemingway 159.
30. See Peter Lisca, 'The Structure of Hemingway's *Across the River and into the Trees,' Modern Fiction Studies* (Summer, 1966), 248.
31. Ernest Hemingway, *Across the River and into the Trees* (Penguin edition, 1966), 38.
32. Hemingway 19.
33. Hemingway 21.
34. Hemingway 36.
35. Hemingway 38.
36. Hemingway 43.
37. Hemingway 93.
38. Hemingway 63.
39. Hemingway 118
40. Hemingway 85-86 & 89.
41. Hemingway 67.
42. Ernest Hemingway, *Islands in the Stream* (Bantam Books, 1971), 4.

Appendix

(A) THE STORY OF *THE OLD MAN AND THE SEA*

IN HIS critique of *The Old Man and the Sea* in *Hemingway: The Writer as Artist* (Princeton, 1956), 289-320, Carlos Baker says something very useful about the story of this novel. He says:

> In its main outlines, the story is simple in the extreme. Stripped, like the marlin, down to its bare bones, it looks not unlike the 200-word version which Hemingway first recorded in an article on the Gulf Stream during the spring of 1936. An old man fishing alone in a skiff out of Cabanas hooked a great marlin that, on the heavy sash-cord handline, pulled the skiff far out to sea. Two days later, the old man was picked up by fishermen 60 miles to the eastward, the head and forward part of the marlin lashed alongsided What was left of the fish, less than half, weighed 800 pounds. The old man has stayed with him a day, a night, a day and another night while the fish swam deep and pulled the boat. When he had come up, the old man had pulled the boat up on him and harpooned him. Lashed alongside the sharks had hit him and the old man had fought them alone in the Gulf Stream in a skiff, clubbing them, stabbing at them, lunging at them with an oar until he was exhausted and the sharks had eaten all they could hold. He was crying in the boat when the fishermen picked him up, half crazy from his loss, and the sharks were still circling the boat.
>
> The difference between this anecdote and the finished work of art is of course immense. What makes the difference is the manner of narration.

(B) *THE GARDEN OF EDEN*

Hemingway's posthumously-published book, *The Garden of Eden* (New York, 1986), is a novel of 247 pages. It is divided into four Books, and it contains thirty chapters. Book I of this novel contains three chapters; Book II has five chapters; Book III consists of sixteen chapters, while Book IV of this novel has six chapters in it. Book I may be considered as Introduction or Exposition; Book II projects the intensity of the drama of love going on in the novel at a higher pitch; Book III registers the presence of evil in the form of perversity, disillusionment and jealousy, while the last Book records an extension of the drama of love, though the persons, participating in it, have changed their positions and attitudes.

By the middle of the novel, the love motif gets weaker and is substituted by the art motif, by a commitment to writing.

The hero of *The Garden of Eden* is David, a writer and a good-natured person. The other two important characters in this novel are Catherine, David's wife, and Marita. It is the action of and interaction among these three characters that form the plot of this novel.

Although Catherine is a rather crazy woman, David and she are happy in their garden of Eden until such time as evil sneaks into it, not really by way of Marita, but in the form of emotional torture and psychic wound. Symbolically speaking, David is the innocent Adam who succumbs to the wiles and stratagems of his wife, Catherine, endearingly called the devil.

(C) SYMBOLISM IN HEMINGWAY'S SHORT STORIES

The first volume of Hemingway's short stories published in 1925 is *In Our Time*. Later, all the short stories contained in this volume were published, along with 'The Snows of Kilimanjaro,' as *The Snows of Kilimanjaro and Other Stories* in 1963. The next volume of Hemingway's short stories to come out in 1927 is *Men Without Women*. The third collection of his short stories was published in 1933 as *Winner Take Nothing*. However, the short stories included in this volume, along with 'The Short Happy Life of Francis Macomber,' were published as *The Short Happy Life of Francis Macomber and Other Stories* in 1963. Yet another collection of Hemingway's short stories, *The Fifth*

Column and the First Forty-Nine Stories, came out in 1938, which, besides containing all his short stories published earlier, contains a few short stories not published till then. The last volume of his short stories captioned *The Fifth Column and Four Stories of the Spanish Civil War* came out posthumously in 1969.

Fifteen of Hemingway's stories are based on the life of Nicholas Adams, supposedly a literary version of the young Hemingway himself. These stories are : 'Indian Camp;' 'The Doctor and the Doctor's Wife;' 'The Battler;' 'The Killers;' 'Ten Indians;' 'The End of Something;' 'The Three-Day Blow;' 'Big Two-Hearted River;' 'In Another Country;' 'A Very Short Story;' 'Cross Country Snow;' 'The Light of the World;' 'Now I lay Me;' 'A Way You'll Never Be;' and 'Fathers and Sons.' Five of them tell us about young men, and they are 'The Revolutionist;' 'My Old Man;' 'God Rest You Merry, Gentlemen;' 'A Day's Wait' and 'The Capital of the World.' Another twelve of them are the stories of war and love, and they are: 'On the Quai at Smyrna;' 'The Soldier's Home;' 'A Natural History of the Dead;' 'Up in Michigan;' 'Out of Season;' 'Mr. And Mrs. Elliot;' 'Cat in the Rain;' 'A Canary for One;' 'An Alpine Idyll;' 'Hills like White Elephants;' 'The Sea Change' and 'Homage to Switzerland.' Yet another eleven of them offer us the stories of the underworld and these short stories are 'A Simple Enquiry;' 'A Pursuit Race;' 'Banal Story;' 'After the Storm;' 'The Mother of a Queen;' 'Wine of Wyoming;' 'One Reader Writes;' 'The Gambler, the Nun, and the Radio;' 'A Clean, Well-Lighted Place;' 'Two Tales of Darkness;' and 'Get a Seeing Eyed Dog.' Three of Hemingway's short stories, namely, 'The Undefeated,' 'Fifty Grand' and 'Today is Friday,' are those of courage and endurance, while another two of them, such as 'Che Ti Dice La Patria' and 'A Meal in Spezia' deal with the menace of Fascism. And while four of his short stories namely, 'The Denunciation;' 'The Butterfly and the Tank;' 'Night before Battle,' and 'Under the Ridge,' take us straight on to the Spanish Civil War, another three of them, 'Old Man at the Bridge,' 'The Short Happy Life of Francis Macomber' and 'The

Snows of Kilimanjaro,' mark the consummation of Hemingway's narrative art.

If we come across women with dead babies and mules with broken forelegs in 'On the Quai at Smyrna,' pointing to the disorder and cruelty of war, we do also notice the pregnancy of the waitress and of Nick's wife in 'Cross Country Snow,' suggesting a strange kind of sadness in the case of both. Moreover, the empty bottle and empty glasses in this story imply the emotional vacuity of both Nick and George. The blinds behind which Nick's mother takes refuge symbolize the spiritual and moral state of this character who refuses to come out of her groove and face reality. The deserted mill in 'The End of Something' stands for the imminent break of love-relationship between Nick and Marjorie. In 'The Battler' the mutilated face of Ad Francis symbolizes his deformed mental state. The wife's desire in 'Cat in the Rain' to have a cat and to grow her hair acquires a symbolical significance in the sense that it reflects her craving for womanhood and affection. In 'Up in Michigan,' the mist coming up from the bay anticipates the bleak relationship between Jim and Liz. The wind blowing for three days in 'The Three-Day Blow' serves as an agent of destruction in the story, while the camp, the swamp and the sport of fishing in 'Big Two-Hearted River' acquire the value of home, the function of a death-trap and the quality of bliss respectively in this story. Similarly, it is the wind mixed with snow that serves as a symbol of confusion or muddle in 'In Another Country.' And while the symbols of light and darkness are properly employed in 'Now I Lay Me,' they are suitably developed in 'A Clean, Well-Lighted Place.'

In 'A Canary for One,' the canary itself works as a symbol: it stands for the American lady's untrained mind. In 'Hills like White Elephants,' it is for six times that hills are described as white elephants in the story, and this picture of hills as white elephants represents not merely the girl's pregnancy or her awaited motherhood, but also her fear of losing her lover. In 'A Simple Enquiry,' the snow stands for the abnormal, while in

'Ten Indians,' unlike in 'The Three-Day Blow,' the wind is projected as an agent of cleansing or purgation. In 'After the Storm,' the storm and the wreckage of a ship symbolize death and destruction. The radio in 'The Gambler, the Nun and the Radio' symbolizes relief from nada, while in 'Old Man at the Bridge' if the goats represent helpless, simple folk who cannot escape the destruction of war, the cat symbolizes smart, cunning people.

In 'The Snows of Kilimanjaro,' Hemingway makes an abundant use of images and symbols. The big birds in this story are the agents of death and destruction: the hyena symbolizes danger and risk; the snow on the peak of Kilimanjaro stands for immortality of art, while the carcass of a leopard represents the attempt of an artist who has tried to reach the peak of art, but has failed.

It is really interesting to see that a large number of these images and symbols have been used in Hemingway's novels too.

(D)

The Torrents of Spring (1926) is Hemingway's first exercise in longer fiction. While the title of this novel has been borrowed from Turgenev's novel, *Spring Torrents*, really speaking, this work is a burlesque, for it is an attack on Sherwood Anderson and also on Gertrude Stein and others of the Paris Circle.

Symbolically speaking, the writing of this novel is a kind of exercise in self-purgation, for it is with *The Torrents of Spring* that Hemingway declares his independence from other writers and tries to assert his identity as an artist.

Bibliography

A. PRIMARY SOURCE

Hemingway, E., *Green Hills of Africa* (Perma Books edition, 1956).

——, *Men Without Women* (Penguin edition, 1962).

——, *In our Time* (included in *The Snows of Kilimanjaro and Other Stories*, Penguin edition, 1963).

——, *Winner Take Nothing* (included in *The Short Happy Life of Francis Macomber and Other Stories*, Penguin edition, 1963).

——, *For Whom the Bell Tolls* (Penguin edition, 1964).

——, *The Torrents of Spring* (Penguin edition, 1966).

——, *Death in the Afternoon* (Penguin edition, 1966).

——, *The Fifth Column* (Penguin edition, 1966).

——, *Across the River and into the Trees* (Penguin edition, 1966).

——, *A Moveable Feast* (Penguin edition, 1966).

——, *The Old Man and the Sea* (Moscow, 1967).

——, *To Have and Have Not* (Penguin edition, 1969).

——, *Islands in the Stream* (New York, 1970).

——, *By Line: Ernest Hemingway* (Penguin edition, 1970).

——, *The Sun Also Rises* (Penguin edition, 1974).

——, *The Essential Hemingway* (Penguin edition, 1974).

——, *A Farewell to Arms* (Penguin edition, 1975).

——, *Ernest Hemingway: Selected Letters*, ed. Carlos Baker (New York, 1981).

——, *The Garden of Eden* (New York, 1986).

B. SECONDARY SOURCE

(i) Books

Aldridge, J.W., *After the Lost Generation: A Critical Study of the Writers of Two Wars* (New York, 1951).

Allen, Walter, *Tradition and Dream: The English and American Novels from the Twenties to Our Time* (London, 1964).

Assilineau, Roger, *The Literary Reputation of Hemingway in Europe* (New York, 1965).

Atkins, John, *The Art of Ernest Hemingway* (New York, 1952).

Baker, Carlos, *Hemingway: The Writer as Artist* (Princeton, 1956).

——, *Hemingway and His Critics: An International Anthology* (New York, 1961).

Baker, Carlos (ed.) *Ernest Hemingway: Critiques of Four Major Novels* (New York, 1962).

——, *Ernest Hemingway: A Life Story* (New York, 1969).

Baker, Sheridan, *Ernest Hemingway: An Introduction and Interpretation* (New York, 1967).

Benson, J.J. (ed.) *The Short Stories of Ernest Hemingway: Critical Essays* (Duke, 1975).

Brown, John (ed.) *Hemingway* (New York, 1961).

Buckley, Peter, *Ernest Hemingway* (New York, 1978).

Burgess, Anthony, *Ernest Hemingway and his World* (New York, 1978).

Chase, Richard, *The American Novel and Its Tradition* (New York, 1957).

Cournas, John, *Famous Modern American Novelists* (New York, 1952).

Fenton, C.A., *The Apprenticeship of Ernest Hemingway: The Early Years* (New York, 1954).

Geismar, Maxwell, *American Moderns: From Rebellion to Conformity* (New York, 1958)

Hoffman, H.J., *The Modern Novel in America* (Chicago, 1951).

Killinger, John, *Hemingway and the Dead Gods: A Study in Existentialism* (Kentucky, 1960).

Lee, A. Robert (ed.) *Ernest Hemingway: New Critical Essays* (New York, 1983).

Lee, Samuels (ed.) *A Hemingway Checklist* (New York, 1951).

Litz, A.W. (ed.) *Modern American Fiction: Essays in Criticism* (New York, 1963)

Machlin, Milt, *The Private Hell of Hemingway* (New York 1962).

Mecaffery, John K.M. (ed.) *Ernest Hemingway: The Man and His Work* (New York, 1950).

Meyers, Jeffrey (ed.) *Hemingway: The Critical Essays* (Boston, 1982).

Nahal, Chaman, *The Narrative Pattern in Ernest Hemingway's Fiction* (Delhi, 1971).

O'Connor, W.V. (ed.) *Seven Modern American Novelists: An Introduction* (New York, 1964).

O'Faslain, Sean, *The Vanishing Hero* (London, 1956).

Rovit, Earl, *Ernest Hemingway* (New York, 1963).

Sanderson, S., *Ernest Hemingway* (London, 1962).

Shaw, Samuel, *Ernest Hemingway* (New York, 1973).

Wagenknecht, Edward, *Cavalcade of the American Novel* (Calcutta, 1969).

Wagner, L.W. (ed.) *Ernest Hemingway: Five Decades of Criticism* (Michigan, 1974).

Waldharn, Arthur (ed.) *Ernest Hemingway: A Collection of Criticism* (New York, 1973).

Weeks, R.P. (ed.) *Hemingway: A Collection of Critical Essays* (Englewood Cliffs: N.J., 1962).

Williams, Wirt, *The Tragic Art of Ernest Hemingway* (Louisiana, 1987).

Young, Philip, *Ernest Hemingway* (New York, 1952).

——, *Ernest Hemingway: A Reconsideration* (Pennysylvania, 1966).

(ii) Journals

Anderson, Charles R., 'Hemingway's Other Style,' *Modern Language Notes*, lxxxvi (May 1961).

Backman, Melvin, 'Hemingway: The Matador and the Crucified,' *Modern Fiction Studies*, i (August 1955).

Burhans Jr., Clinton S., '*The Old Man and the Sea*: Hemingway's Tragic Vision of Man,' *American Literature*, xxxi (January, 1960).

Dupee, F.W., 'Hemingway Revealed,' *Kenyon Review*, xv (Winter, 1953).

Eby, Cecil D., 'The Real Robert Jordan,' *American Literature* (November, 1966).

Engstrom, A.G., 'Dante, Flaubert and "The Snows of Kilimanjaro,"' *Modern Language Notes* (March 1950).

Evans, O., 'The Protagonist of Hemingway's "The Killers,"' *Modern Language Notes* (December 1958).

——, 'The Arrow Wounds of Count Mippipopolous,' *P.M.L.A.* (March, 1962).

Friedrich, O., '*A Farewell to Arms*,' *The American Scholar*, xxvi (1956).

Graham, John, 'Ernest Hemingway: The Meaning of Style,' *Modern Fiction Studies*, vi (Winter, 1960).

Halliday, E.M., 'Hemingway's Narrative Perspective,' *The Sewanee Review*, ix (Spring, 1952).

Halliday, E.M., 'Hemingway's Ambiguity: Symbolism and Irony,' *American Literature*, xxvii (March 1956).

Hattam, Edward, 'Hemingway's "An Alpine Idyll,"' *Modern Fiction Studies* (Summer, 1966).

Modern Fiction Studies, Vol. I (August 1955) contains essays on

Hemingway by Melvin Backman, Tom Burnam, C. Hugh Holman, Bernard S. Oldsey, H.K. Russell, and Green D. Wyrick.

Lisca, Peter, 'The Structure of Hemingway's "*Across the River and into the Trees*,"' *Modern Fiction Studies* (Summer, 1966).

Light, James F., 'The Religion of Death in *A Farewell to Arms*,' *Modern Fiction Studies*, vii (Summer, 1961).

Schorer, Mark, 'The Background of a Style,' *Kenyon Review*, iii (Winter, 1941).

——, 'With Grace under Pressure,' *New Republic* cxxvii, (Oct. 6, 1952).

Stephens, R.O., 'Hemingway's Riddle of Kilimanjaro: Idea and Image,' *American Literature* (March 1960).

——, 'Hemingway's The Old Man and the Iceberg,' *Modern Fiction Studies*, vii (Winter 1961-62).

Sylvester, Bickford, 'Hemingway's Extended Vision: *The Old Man and the Sea*,' *P.M.L.A.*, lxxxi (March 1966).

Young, P., 'Hemingway and Me: A Rather Long Story,' *Kenyon Review*, xxviii (January 1966).